Reaching for the Knowledge Edge

Reaching for the Knowledge Edge

How the Knowing Corporation
Seeks, Shares & Uses Knowledge
for Strategic Advantage

Kenneth J. Hatten
Stephen R. Rosenthal

AMACOM
American Management Association
New York • Atlanta • Boston • Chicago • Kansas City • San Francisco • Washington, D. C.
Brussels • Mexico City • Tokyo • Toronto

Special discounts on bulk quantities of AMACOM books are available to corporations, professional associations, and other organizations. For details, contact Special Sales Department, AMACOM, a division of American Management Association, 1601 Broadway, New York, NY 10019.
Tel.: 212-903-8316. Fax: 212-903-8083.
Web site: www.amacombooks.org

This publication is designed to provide accurate and authoritative information in regard to the subject matter covered. It is sold with the understanding that the publisher is not engaged in rendering legal, accounting, or other professional service. If legal advice or other expert assistance is required, the services of a competent professional person should be sought.

Library of Congress Cataloging-in-Publication Data

Hatten, Kenneth J.
    Reaching for the knowledge edge : how the knowing corporation seeks, shares & uses knowledge for strategic advantage / Kenneth J. Hatten, Stephen R. Rosenthal.
    p. cm.
    Includes bibliographical references and index.
    ISBN 0-8144-0634-3
    1. Knowledge management.   2. Strategic planning.
    I. Rosenthal, Stephen R.   II. Title.
    HD30.2.H386   2001
    658.4'038—dc21   00–068255

© 2001 Kenneth J. Hatten and Stephen R. Rosenthal.
All rights reserved.
Printed in the United States of America.

This publication may not be reproduced,
stored in a retrieval system,
or transmitted in whole or in part,
in any form or by any means, electronic,
mechanical, photocopying, recording, or otherwise,
without the prior written permission of AMACOM,
a division of American Management Association,
1601 Broadway, New York, NY 10019.

Printing number

10 9 8 7 6 5 4 3 2 1

To our wives—**Mary Louise** and
Linda—and our families,
whose humor and counsel continue
to inspire us

Contents

Preface *ix*

1. "Knowing": Getting Real about *Knowledge Management*   1
2. Aligning Action with the Customer   19
3. Checking Feasibility: Customers, Capabilities, and Competencies   47
4. Understanding Strategic Stretch   79
5. Managing Stretch Risks   107
6. Experimenting to Build Competencies   135
7. Using the Performance Measurement System   161
8. Getting Everyone Involved: A Knowing Culture   193
9. Leading with Knowledge: A Personal Agenda   215

Selected References   *231*

Index   *235*

Preface

This book emerged from several partnerships we participated in during the past four years. Listing the partnerships here provides an understanding of the origins of the ideas and tools presented in the book. In our case, doing this is more than a publication tradition. It is also a micro example of the main theme of the book: creating productive processes for seeking, sharing, and refining practical knowledge.

First, consider the partnership between us, the two authors. The book itself is a strong argument for synergy based on diversity, because each of us brought different expertise, problem-solving styles, and communications skills to this project. This diversity, we believe, enriched the learning process as we developed our models and concepts, tested them in many executive forums and MBA classrooms, and then refined them through multiple drafts of our book manuscript. Over time, we dramatically improved the effectiveness with which we worked together, as we increasingly appreciated each other's base of experience and skills, and gained confidence in using our new frames and concepts as a basis for communication and problem solving.

Next, consider the interplay between theory and practice. The origins of many of the ideas in this book came from an ongoing dialogue with a cadre of executives who are members of the Center for Enterprise Leadership at Boston University. Some years ago, Fred Purdue, vice president and general manager for reengineering at Pitney

Bowes, asked us if we could shift our research agenda from the traditional concerns of operations managers and product development executives to a whole-enterprise point of view. We polled the corporate members of our research center, and they agreed that the most critical need was for new practical frameworks to help them participate more effectively in their companies' strategy formulation and knowledge management processes. They were beginning to work cross-functionally, and expressed concern that because they were under pressure to perform, they had to find ways to learn in action. They believed that the wave of reengineering had already yielded the low-hanging fruit, and that something more was now needed.

At about the same time, Boston University School of Management asked us to develop a new course that would evaluate the movement to cross-functional management across global industries. Dean Louis E. Lataif had long been a proponent of cross-functional management, and had made this a curriculum priority at the school. Our colleagues, Professors Lloyd Baird, John Henderson, and N. Venkatraman, were making interesting discoveries in the emerging field of knowledge management. So we committed ourselves to a program of research that focused on current theory and practice with a simple objective—to find a way to help operating managers of all types participate in their companies' strategy debates, and move their companies closer to the knowledge edge that yields a competitive advantage.

The ideas in this book were developed during several years of interaction and testing with executive groups from the Center for Enterprise Leadership and in other organizations. We cannot individually thank each person who participated in this process, but we would like to single out the following: Fred Purdue at Pitney Bowes, whose support has been considerable and constant; Lance Hall, director of supply chain strategy and engineering at Colgate-Palmolive, who opened so many doors for our research and has long been an advocate for putting the customer first; Joerg Schreiber, vice president of research and development at Roche Diagnostics, who helped us understand the difference between knowledge creation and knowledge sharing; Gerry Angeli, vice president of OEM supply business at Concord Camera, whose knowledge of performance measurement helped us to see the power of practical measures in implementing strategy; and Shirley Blanch, executive consultant/change specialist at Johnson & Johnson Ethicon, who tested our models in her company and introduced many of our colleagues to our ideas.

Thanks are also due to our colleagues at Boston University, Jeff Miller, whose ideas on the knowledge initiation process shaped ours, N. Venkatraman, Len Johnson, and Dan Dimancescu, who were there at the beginning. Michael Shwartz, James Post, and Carol Hoopes kindly reviewed early drafts of our manuscript and provided helpful advice. Many of our former students, now successful MBAs, helped us to learn through their efforts. We apologize to anyone whose contribution we have not acknowledged and take full responsibility for any errors or omissions.

Adrienne Hickey, our acquisitions editor at AMACOM, has a keen eye and uses a direct style. She made this publication project a pleasure. Some of our ideas also benefited from excellent editorial reviews by *Long Range Planning, Strategic Communication Management,* and *Knowledge Management Review,* where Rowan Wilson, in particular, earned our gratitude.

Finally, we thank our wives, Mary Louise Hatten and Linda Rosenthal, who—sometimes cheerfully, sometimes not—tolerated our absences from family matters as we pressed toward publication.

> Kenneth J. Hatten and Stephen R. Rosenthal
> Boston
> September 2000

*Reaching
for the
Knowledge
Edge*

1
"Knowing": Getting Real about *Knowledge Management*

At the dawn of the twentieth century, there were pundits who confidently proclaimed that "All that can be invented, is invented" and "Man will never fly." Now, as we enter the twenty-first century, this sense of limits seems to have disappeared. The conventional wisdom is one of confidence that new inventions and better ways to do things will continue to be discovered, despite the incredible accomplishments to date.

As individuals, most of us realize that we can prepare for change by increasing our awareness of what we do or do not know. As we sense gaps in our own knowledge, we become more open to learning. Our personal experience confirms that change is one of the constant realities of our lives and that as we deal with the possibility of change, small decisions can have big effects. Some of us, upon reflection, have observed that we must have curiosity if we are to learn.

Moving from our personal lives to our organizational lives, what does this sense of the future signify? Think about the shift in the nature of leadership. In all but the smallest of companies, the chief executive officer (CEO) alone cannot know enough to call all the shots. Rapid change and uncertainty in markets, technologies, and the structure of industries generate new opportunities for organizations that are able to create, develop, and apply new knowledge. Doing this well depends on the cooperation and creativity of the many people who have ongoing operational responsibilities. As John Brown, British Petroleum's CEO in 1997, said: "To generate extraordinary value for shareholders, a company has to learn better than its competitors and apply that knowledge throughout its businesses faster and more widely than they do."[1]

Still, why the fuss about knowledge? The familiar answer to this question is that knowledge is the only sustainable source of competitive advantage, as stated more than twenty years ago by Ray Stata, president and CEO of Analog Devices. Less appreciated, but even more significant, is Peter Drucker's observation: "Knowledge constantly makes itself obsolete. . . . And the knowledge that matters is subject to rapid and abrupt shifts."[2] Because in business, as well as in the sciences, knowledge itself is ever changing. Therefore, there can be considerable value gained from timely action when it is aimed at confronting uncertainties directly, and then learning from this process. But to learn as we go, we have to move ahead with purpose—that is, we have to focus our learning where it counts. We have to know what we are trying to learn. We have to mesh learning with purpose.

This book is about mastering the management of two types of knowledge. First, the knowledge you need to boost your performance when you know your organizational objectives. Second, the knowledge that will help you define new objectives and the strategies to pursue them. Pursuing both types of knowledge is essential if you want to gain a competitive edge in your industry.

An Overview of This Book

This book will help you and your management team become business leaders by creating new know-how, using it, and reaping its rewards. While followers imitate where they can, and struggle where they cannot, you will be able to pay attention to what you know, how you use it, and how you expand it. The approach you will learn here includes:

- The types of knowledge that must be *shared* to align strategic objectives with operational reality
- The types of knowledge needed to reach further, to *stretch* and exploit your capabilities and capacity, to accelerate growth and to boost profitability
- A process for constructively influencing others in your organization as you *seek* the new knowledge needed to strengthen and renew your business

The first category, *sharing* knowledge, affects every manager. Staying efficient and effective in your current markets requires leaders to fuse strategy with the operating system, thereby creating a dynamic loop where capability is enhanced and performance improved. We will leave behind the outmoded traditional notions that strategy and operations are divorced in both thought and deed, and that strategy is best formulated and executed in multiyear cycles by single executives acting independently of each other. In the knowledge economy, it is more useful to signal and test strategies in action rather than freezing them in formal multiyear plans. Corporate leaders must create organizations that can strategize as they work, and work as they strategize. Doing this well requires the types of knowledge-sharing that we describe in Chapters 2 and 3.

The second category, *stretching* with knowledge to hand, is of great concern to managers who play some role in shaping strategy, since they then need to work with others to identify opportunities in which their organization's competencies and capabilities can be deployed to advantage. It is also important for managers who choose to contract or partner with other organizations as a cost-effective way to build a customer-serving enterprise. This requires explicit awareness of what your organization already knows and how it might be put to its highest and best use in present and potential markets. It also requires sufficient knowledge of the business environment to be able to ask where else you could successfully compete, grow, and boost your productivity and profitability. To make the right choices from among the options you identify, you will need to assess your company's ability to manage its inherent risks. Chapters 4 and 5 give you the tools you need for applying knowledge and creating—and then realistically assessing—future business scenarios.

The third category, mastering the process of *seeking* new knowledge in action, involves all managers who have a part to play in this process—not just the few senior managers who may work top-down to fundamentally change their organization's culture. Competitive success flows to companies whose leaders learn to adapt by routinely listening to their external environment, customers, and key employees. Employees can be valuable sources of knowledge if they pay attention to what is going on and are able to ask effective questions that shape thinking and action in their companies.

Learning in action through deliberate experiments is a powerful approach when leaders are comfortable in stretching their organizations to seize opportunities beyond their grasp. Not every experiment works out as planned, but they serve to limit the financial and organizational risks of change as they create new opportunities. Such organizational experiments should be initiated and expanded to continuously test market dynamics and new venture possibilities, while developing your organization's knowledge base, executives, and new sources of advantage. In sum, management needs to trigger strategic learning—that is, learning not just within the comfort zone of the company's current customers, capabilities, and competencies but beyond them. This strategy requires influencing other people in your organization by using carefully selected performance measures, combined with a process of building coalitions for action based on the knowledge gained. Chapters 6 through 8 show you how to do this. Chapter 9 offers related suggestions for your own personal agenda.

Taken as a whole, this book is designed to help you be a leader in your company's quest to make knowledge management real. It will help you to do your current job better. It will also prepare you to play a key role in determining future directions for your company, perhaps beyond the scope of your current responsibilities. Before we move on to these tested approaches, let us review the new context of management in which *knowing* is a central pursuit.

The New Context of Leadership: The Need to Know

Knowledge matters to competitive success, in part, because the basis of so many businesses is changing. Much of this change is driven by new technological possibilities. As the field of photography transitions from capturing images on film to digital formats, Kodak needs to adapt. Chemistry was once a core component of that company, but now it needs to be knowledgeable about electronics as well. Microsoft built its success on building software for personal computer (PC) operating systems, but now it needs to be at the forefront of Internet applications. Amazon.com started as a virtual bookstore, but at this writing considers itself to be in a much broader multiproduct consumer business. The knowledge economy has stimulated many manufacturing companies to develop related services, and other companies to think in terms of providing information of value to their customers. All of these shifts bring an accompanying need for new knowledge.

One result of such dramatic change in technological and market opportunity is that never before are so many senior executives asking, "What business is our company in?" and "What business should we be in?" Similar questions are on the minds of managers everywhere: "How *could* changes in the global economy affect the future of my industry and this company?" "How *should* we exploit the Internet?" "Do shifts in the economic landscape require new forms of business leadership?" "How do these changes affect my own day-to-day practices as a business leader?"

Some executives say, "Times may change but the essence of leading a company like mine doesn't." Still, other executives state, "Once the new trends emerge, leaders will know what to do to be successful in that new business climate." We believe both of these responses are incorrect. We *are* in a new economy where sustaining competitive leadership calls for radically different modes of thinking, learning, and action. The winners will be those companies that lead and learn before the other companies do, rather than those that fruitlessly wait for the comfort of stable trends to emerge.

The types of knowledge required go far beyond the realm of new-to-the-world emerging technologies, and include products, services, markets, and management processes. For example, although it is true that new telecommunications technology and the Internet have changed the size of the potential market for most organizations and enabled them to participate in the global economy, there are other types of knowledge that are necessary for their success. During the past ten years, companies of all types quickly expanded the geographic boundaries of their businesses, whether they were ready to do so or not. Some companies were successful, but many were frustrated and forced to retreat. We have learned that attempting to sell products or services to worldwide markets is not necessarily a recipe for profitable growth. Global companies face complexities that demand new and specialized knowledge. For example, management needs to understand local customer requirements and design global products and services with these local needs in mind. It has to procure components, materials, and services on a global basis to achieve heightened economies of scale and to learn how to quickly transfer best practices from its region of origin to other parts of the world.

Given these complexities and the varieties of new knowledge needed, we have had to learn once again that "Fire! Ready! Aim!" does not work. Feedback from customers, process-by-process and across all the business processes, can inform strategy and signal the direction of change. Strategically driven information technology (IT) investments can be crucial in executing these process redesigns, but we have all seen examples of IT investments that were wasteful and fell short of their initial promise. Information technology investments are warranted if they are directed by managers who understand how their new process designs are created to improve service in the customer's eyes and who can leverage IT's power to deliver those services better, faster, easier, and cheaper.

The real winners in the emerging new economy will be individuals and companies that make "knowing" a living reality throughout their organizations and develop the ability to reach for the competitive edge that only new knowledge can sustain. Knowing corporations are those led by operating managers of every rank and variety who have learned to live at the knowledge edge.

"Knowing" and Knowledge Management

Knowledge-building efforts need to be directed toward improving business performance and identifying new business opportunities and competitively advantaged strategies. Therefore, your quest for knowledge must be purposeful.

▲ British Petroleum (now BP Amoco) set out to cut its drilling costs to make long known oil fields economical. By identifying who knew what, where they were, and how to access them, BP developed a knowledge-sharing process using its company intranet to host a network of company, partner, and supplier experts to tap existing but widely scattered knowledge within this greater drilling enterprise. In this way, BP cut its drilling costs in half, developed better operating procedures, and was able to eliminate expensive operating shutdowns.

▲ The United States Army needed to respond to the demands of new and complex missions during a period of tightened budgets. The Army used knowledge management and new information technology to maintain its battlefield readiness and flexibility. Technology and information helped the Army to meet these objectives by cutting its materials consumption and waste, the size of its forces, and the cost of its supply lines. Some of its efficiency gains were due to the adoption of smart weapons. Some were due to new information systems that delivered battlefield intelligence throughout the army in real time, thereby allowing a shared view of the battlefield. However, much of the gain was due to methods and training developed at the Center for Army Lessons Learned (CALL), particularly the revival of after-action reviews (AARs) that are designed to improve battlefield decision processes at every level within the Army. These new processes helped the Army to turn data into knowledge, share the knowledge it had, stretch its capabilities, and create new knowledge and capabilities.

In the knowing corporation, knowledge-based initiatives have the same agenda: Share what you have so you can use it. Stretch what you have to become more productive and competitive. Create new knowledge to develop a competitive edge in any business process that deals with acquiring and serving customers. Because your company already has executives responsible for achieving business objectives and improving performance, there is limited need for special cadres of knowledge management executives and a staff with a special budget. Nor do you need to invent some new, arcane knowledge management jargon that may become the next gag in Scott Adams's *Dilbert* comic strip.

Instead, this book shows you how to integrate doing business with a purposeful search for knowledge. The knowledge you gain from action and its outcomes will inform not only your current operations, but also help you to define new business opportunities and strategies. For successful managers who want to be considered as true leaders in their company, being part of this ongoing knowledge creation and application process is not optional. In a knowing corporation, leaders at every organizational level need to combine being practical—that is, being focused on the achievement of their current business objectives—with being venturesome and keeping a strategic eye out for opportunity.

Like any other corporation, a knowing corporation must have a purpose, objectives, and strategies. However, a knowing corporation distinguishes itself from the pack because its managers and leaders of every rank repeatedly come to grips with the key question, *What knowledge matters (to this organization)?* Its people have learned to convert the results of their ongoing business and other new discoveries into knowledge and insights, which they share with others. As a result, their organization is a self-aware, adaptive, and continuously improving competitor.

Questions are the key to perfecting an organization's ability to learn from action. Accordingly, this book provides sets of questions that need to be asked and points to ways in which you can reach for your answers—answers that fit your corporate and business situation, and the context within which you manage, whether sharing, stretching, or seeking knowledge is your immediate priority. These questions and approaches will trigger the learning that your organization needs to test and build its knowledge, whether it is an ongoing business, new venture, or new alliance.

The Creation of Knowledge from Action

Consider how knowledge emerges from action in the business world. Recall the fears of a Y2K crisis. Rather than simply dismissing the pre-2000 alarms as a fraud and our preparations as waste, realize that the calm the world experienced in passing into the twenty-first century has a cause. Crises can be avoided by facing reality, sizing up the situation, sharing information, planning a response, and investing to make things work out. This same calm, action-based yet reflective approach can also serve us well in a corporation on an ongoing basis rather than "once-in-a-millennium," either when we see things changing or when we are surprised by unanticipated change from new forms of competition or by our customers' responses. Building and sustaining a competitive advantage requires vigilance and continuous effort, imagination and insight, all brought together by the knowing corporation.

Despite uncertainties about markets and competition, the new beginning will be an initial set of insights about the direction and pace of external change, the shape and size of new business opportunities, and the capabilities and competencies needed to win. We make no claim that learning will eliminate business uncertainty or risk. Surprises will be frequent and often confusing, even when there is considerable imagination and energy dedicated to getting and staying ahead. What we need are approaches to help us deal with the present *and* future simultaneously, to help us become more customer-centered and ensure that our operations are infused with strategy, and to help us develop the organizational competencies we will need to open and retain new markets.

Ironically, it is time for a return to the basics, but with a twist. For example, although most companies pay lip service to being customer-centered, they have yet to make this a reality. This occurs because it is difficult to align an organization's customer-visible business processes to serve its customers with quick reengineering initiatives, which usually fail to achieve this critical objective. Yet customer-centering is a critical building block and can become a foundation for learning in action and then sharing the new knowledge to take further action that will strengthen your operating systems.

More than ever before, preparing your organization for competition means being a member of several groups of engaged managers with the knowledge, skills, and perspectives to work strategically at the enterprise level and simultaneously align the operational core. All participants need to be skilled in sensing strategic signals that ultimately define the strategic realities of their current and future customer relationships. Unfortunately, after years of reengineering, downsizing, and culling executive development expenses, few companies have enough people capable of doing this.

Part of the solution is to gain access to the knowledge of others. The dawning of electronic commerce offered dramatically new networking possibilities to almost every company. The Internet makes it possible to create new partnerships more easily than ever before, and to lever your specialist's partners competencies and process capabilities, thereby creating supply chains that are faster and cheaper to operate. The general question that drives learning in this domain is, "What should our company do itself and what should be done by its contractors and business partners?"

Seven Ways to Sharpen Your Knowledge Edge

Whatever your current job responsibilities may be, this book will help you and your associates to work together to create a knowledge edge that yields competitive advantage. You will learn an integrated set of new approaches that will help you address critical business challenges and opportunities in both the short and long term. Here is a brief description of these seven approaches.

1. *The Action Alignment (AA) Model.* Our first approach centers on your current strategy and its associated operating activities. You will learn the concept of *action alignment* and how to use the AA model to assess your organization's alignment. You will be able to create a new picture of your business, mirroring the way it is perceived by your current customers. The AA model highlights critical questions about the effectiveness of your current orga-

nization and how alignment impacts the effectiveness of your core business processes. This will help you and your management team to sharpen your collective judgment about how well your operating systems and internal business practices are serving your customers. In particular, it will become easier for you to gain consensus on how to prioritize the actions needed to fully realize the potential of your markets and your strategy. Action alignment through targeted knowledge management will become your path to progress.

2. *The Do/Contract Decision.* More than ever before, your company's success is determined by the business partners it selects and how they perform. Careful contracting and partnering will allow you to perform above and beyond what you and your fellow managers could achieve within the resource bounds of your own company. We extend the AA model into the multicompany enterprise zone by structuring the key decision that all enterprise leaders must make: what to do internally and what capacities and capabilities to acquire through partnerships and contracts. You will learn how to address this do/contract decision along with the AA model, combining traditional financial considerations with notions of organizational competencies and proprietary knowledge. Your increased awareness of the implications of this decision will sharpen your own agenda for creating and leveraging knowledge.

3. *The 3C Test for Strategic Balance.* Next, with this larger enterprise point of view in mind, you will learn a simple test to assess the feasibility of your current business strategy. This test simultaneously looks at three critical dimensions of your strategy: the customers you have chosen to target, the business process capabilities that you have achieved, and the organizational competencies (or know-how) that already exist. The 3C test for strategic balance lifts you and your fellow managers above the details of the

AA model to identify critical gaps in your capabilities and competencies. You will have a quick but comprehensive approach for assessing the overall success, across functional lines, of implementing your existing business strategy. This test will help you avoid the knowledge trap faced by the six fabled blind people who could only describe an elephant in terms of the individual elements they could touch—its trunk, its leg, its tail, its ears—rather than its entire being. Instead of such fragmentary knowledge, you will learn the integrative power from appreciating sets of strategic capabilities and competencies and related gaps.

4. *The Strategic Stretch Test.* Next, you will be asked to shift your thinking to the future, where new business opportunities may abound. We extend the notion of 3C balance into the zone of strategy evaluation where an enterprise's knowledge edge can spell the difference between glorious success and a dismal demise. You will learn the strategic stretch test, which is designed to help your organization stretch toward new opportunities without breaking. This test starts with the dimensions of customers, capabilities, and competencies—the 3Cs already introduced—and compares future requirements to what is currently achievable. It then extends into explicit assessments of competitive advantage and competitive surprise, external and internal stakeholders, and the constraints they impose on a company. You will learn how to work with others in your organization to apply this simple yet comprehensive test of strategic feasibility. When your organization decides whether or not to go in a new strategic direction, it will be with the benefit of a knowledge-based assessment of the associated risks and with an awareness of the options that you have for managing them.

5. *The EKG Review.* Once you think in terms of strategic stretch, you will appreciate the need for learning in action. The approach we advise is to design and conduct

strategic experiments aimed at gaining knowledge to support subsequent decisions about which opportunities to pursue, objectives to set, and approaches to adopt. First you will learn the difference between a strategic business experiment and the more common notion of a scientific experiment. Then you will learn how to assess the experimental knowledge gained, or your organization's EKG. The EKG review can help you increase the knowledge gained from your experiments and their action implications. You will also see how the EKG review can add value to your business even when your experiments failed to achieve their initial objectives.

6. *Performance Metrics and Their Use.* Leading companies use organizational performance measures to drive collective action. But the selection of the right set of metrics can be troublesome, particularly during times of strategic change. You will gain new insight into the potential power of such performance measurement systems, which are different from the ones that the human resources department uses to appraise individuals. You will assess the usefulness of your current system and gain new insights into using it purposefully, for example, by widening its scope while increasing its focus. You will learn about setting performance targets and how to deal with other performance measurement problems. With these perspectives in mind, you will be able to add measurement to the arsenal of knowledge-based tools that you have already learned.

7. *The Knowledge Ignition Process.* When a company is fully committed to sharpening its knowledge edge, it will strive to achieve a culture that supports the six approaches previously outlined. More fundamentally, this will also legitimize the kind of innovative knowledge-based behavior that we call the knowledge ignition process. You will learn how to use this process, which is based on cycles of learning in action, and how, ultimately, its repeated use across

your organization can help you to establish a learning culture. You will then learn how to build a case for strategic change while building a coalition of people who will sponsor that change. And you will have the skills to apply the knowledge ignition process proactively, thereby dealing with potential crises and opportunities earlier than your competitors do.

Implications for Leadership

These specific ways to sharpen your knowledge edge are responsive to the demands of the current business environment. Successfully adopting these measures calls for leadership that enthusiastically embraces the dynamic notions of control, which is better suited to the complexities of the knowledge economy than faith in the merits of top-down planning and tight capital and operational budgets. Deliberate speed is more useful for most situations than Internet speed is, but it may seem to present a hopeless paradox. Deliberate speed means we have to stay in motion while leading a revitalization process that is guided by every signal we can catch by listening and learning. It is a delicate process that demands strength and grace, analogous to the movement of a ballerina across a stage. She is in dynamic equilibrium where her motion is the key to maintaining harmony and balance.

Yet the ballerina's performance is substantially different from that of an executive. The ballerina acts within the consistent bounds of a musical score and associated choreography that are fully specified in advance, while the executive is part composer and choreographer—shaping the performance of others—as well as being one of the leading performers. While the world of the ballerina is largely insulated from change, the executive must perform in a world constantly reshaped by social and economic actions and reactions. Thus, unlike the ballerina, the executive must constantly adapt in light of his or her understanding of relevant trends and forces in both the external world and within his or her own organization. Equally important, the executive needs concepts and frameworks that allow others in the organization to join the dance. Finally, and perhaps most importantly, the entire management team occasionally needs to go above the dance floor to the balcony so it can exercise informed leadership of its enterprise. These images of leadership are embodied in the approaches described in this book.

When leaders say "Go!," they formally and fully commit their organization to action. It is a heavy burden. There are standard concepts and measures for retrospectively determining the financial viability of a business enterprise, but few for prospectively evaluating new strategies and their competitive advantage. The earlier that leaders commit to action, the greater the rewards when they are right. The winners in this high-stakes race will be those who can make the right calls when the probabilities of being right versus wrong are 51:49—almost anyone can get the 90:10 stuff right. Luckily, the 51:49 stuff is easier to get right when your decisions are grounded in fact and knowledge—that is, when your organization is committed to learning in action. Welcome to the knowledge economy!

The key to survival and prosperity in this dynamic business environment is not an abstraction called knowledge management, which, if it is declared important in your company, will probably turn out to be someone else's responsibility. Rather, it depends on the ability of every operating manager in your organization to create competitively relevant new knowledge and apply it in his or her decisions. It is new knowledge skillfully used that will strengthen your company's competitive position in its current and future target markets. Collectively, you need to learn from your operations and use the knowledge gained to shape your current strategy while using your strategic experiments to develop tomorrow's. Doing this well requires a set of processes to fuse your operations and strategies now and in the future. Mastering these processes will allow you to become a knowing corporation. This book will show you how to begin.

Notes

1. Steven E. Prokesch, "Unleashing the Power of Learning: An Interview with British Petroleum's John Brown," *Harvard Business Review*, September–October 1997, p. 148.
2. Peter F. Drucker, Esther Dyson, Charles Handy, Paul Saffo, and Peter M. Senge, "Looking Ahead: Implications of the Present," *Harvard Business Review*, September–October 1997, p. 22.

2
Aligning Action with the Customer

The constant striving to meet customer expectations in every way possible is called being *customer-centered*. But unless we make this general concept more tangible—and commit to achieving it—the probable result will be a nice, fuzzy, feel-good, do-good abstraction rather than a state of being. Despite decades of argument by management gurus of every persuasion that the customer must come first, few companies have actually managed to do this.

This chapter offers a framework that will help you and your management team share what you know about your business, its customers, your advantages, and your constraints so you can properly assess the inner workings of your organization. It provides you with a structure that allows you to ask the question, "Who knows what?" Moreover, it will allow your management team to organize what it knows. This is a critical initial step toward consolidating and using your organization's knowledge about both its customers and performance.

The Feel of Alignment

The method we recommend is called *action alignment*. So before we get into the details of this approach, let us get an intuitive feel for the concept of alignment. For a simple alignment experience, put your two hands together for a minute and try making one hand push and one pull. Keep reading!

Most people struggle with this simple task for a short time, placing their hands in conflict either pulling against each other or pushing against each other isometrically until their bodies shake. Then they realize that the first step is to decide which way to go, that is, to set a direction. The choice of "to the left" or "to the right" not only eliminates the conflict but, interestingly, also determines which hand will pull, and which will push. If you move "left," the left hand pulls and the right pushes from behind, and vice versa. It is easier that way, and action flows naturally. Alignment, therefore, allows you to apply the power of each hand for a common purpose.

The point is that alignment flows to purpose. And, just as when we try to align our hands in action, making purpose clear is a problem every manager faces in his or her organization. However, alignment is harder to achieve in organizational life. Consider the "push/pull" exercise again. When we face a room full of executives and tell them, "Go left!," they almost invariably go to *their* left. When we tell them, "No! You've got it all wrong! Go to my left!," they move left in unison. They align themselves quickly once they truly understand our instruction.

Now there is another point to make about achieving aligned action. When we managers say, "Go!," it is our responsibility to make the message and the purpose clear. It is not what we say but what they hear that counts because that directly influences what they do—their actions. After the push/pull exercise, most people get the idea.

"All very well," you might be thinking, "but my organization is far more complex than this." In your organization, people rarely "get the message" all at once. We agree. In your organization, it is very likely that the challenge is not only to get aligned but to stay aligned for a long period of time. Staying aligned, as you know, takes considerable effort across the organization from top to bottom, effort that is not always forthcoming or easily sustained.

Action Alignment: Framework for Customer-Centering

Consider the new product development process for a moment. How is it customer-centered? At both special meetings and on a day-to-day basis, executives from marketing first deal with the product or service idea. It is likely that marketing and technology, often called product engineering, will play the largest roles. Then, conceptual design begins, and, once again, marketing deals with technology and operations, this time to discuss product concepts. As the product or service moves from concept to specification, technology continues to play a large role, but it is necessary to tap operations to ensure feasibility and to build quality into the design. Marketing will join the work on prototype production and testing to ensure that the functionality that customers need is achieved. As the new product development process proceeds toward a manufacturing ramp-up, technology's involvement may recede even as marketing and operations intensify their work together.

Let us think about what is happening here. Consider the real meetings and functional interactions as being the "nodes" where the horizontal new product development process draws on, or crosses, the resources of the vertical functions, marketing, technology, and operations, as indicated in Figure 2-1. For this particular set of nodes, we can now ask the customer-centered question: "Does every function add its knowledge, manpower, and physical resources to the deliberations and decisions at the right time and in the right amounts?"

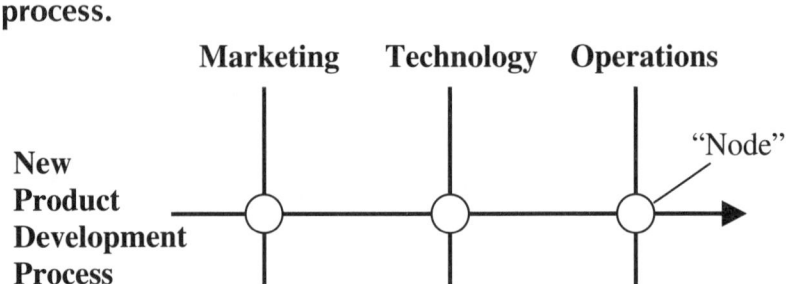

Figure 2-1. An example of a cross-functional business process.

```
              Marketing   Technology   Operations
                  |           |           |
New                                               "Node"
Product      ────○───────────○───────────○──────▶
Development
Process           |           |           |
                  ▼           ▼           ▼
```

These nodes are, of course, imaginary, but the interactions they represent are very real. This is because every node is either an opportunity for a disconnection where things can go wrong or an opportunity for one function or another to make its contributions to the success of the company's new product development effort.

Remember that customers do not care how you manage a business process, they only care about the capabilities you demonstrate on a day-to-day basis. For a customer, only what you consistently deliver counts. Your management teams, therefore, have to design each process and make it work, function by function, and in alignment with all your other business processes. Craig Weatherup said as much when he was president and CEO of Pepsi-Cola North America: "If you don't create structured, repeatable processes, you don't develop long-term capability, and the work doesn't get done."[1]

The principal concern for most managers is to achieve process alignment across business functions and to unify them with a focus on the customer. Any decision or action that impacts the customer is strategic. That is why you need accurate knowledge about the whole network of functions and business processes—how effectively they are reaching the target customer and how efficiently this is being accomplished. Knowledge of this sort needs to be shared by functional and process managers alike to improve performance and get you on your chosen path.

Figure 2-2 illustrates the action alignment model (the AA model), in which we extend the representation of a few functions and one business process to all the functions and all the customer-visible business processes.[2]

The organization is represented, as shown in Figure 2-2, as a network of business functions and processes, graphically portrayed as an interacting set of vertical and horizontal elements. It is a map of the operational core of a business, with functions and processes that have to be aligned to serve customers. The vertical elements are the traditional functions of marketing, technology, and operations, plus the functions that supply resources of every type: human resources management (HRM), information technology (IT), and finance. If you have a different set of functions, custom-label the framework to match your organization by making appropriate substitutions. The AA model is a tool for thinking about your situation, not a sacred, inalterable mystery box handed down by a guru. Nor is it an attempt to illustrate your formal organizational structure. Being customer-centered, it is simply designed to address how things actually work, not who reports to whom.

The second set of AA model elements, the business processes, is represented horizontally. You are already familiar with the notion of these cross-functional processes if your organization lived through the era of business process reengineering (BPR) in the 1990s. The basic concept is that work that directly involves the customer is done through a set of business processes. A common set of labels will be used here: new product development, order acquisition, order fulfillment, post-sales service, and credit and collections. The challenge is to manage these processes

Figure 2-2. The AA model.

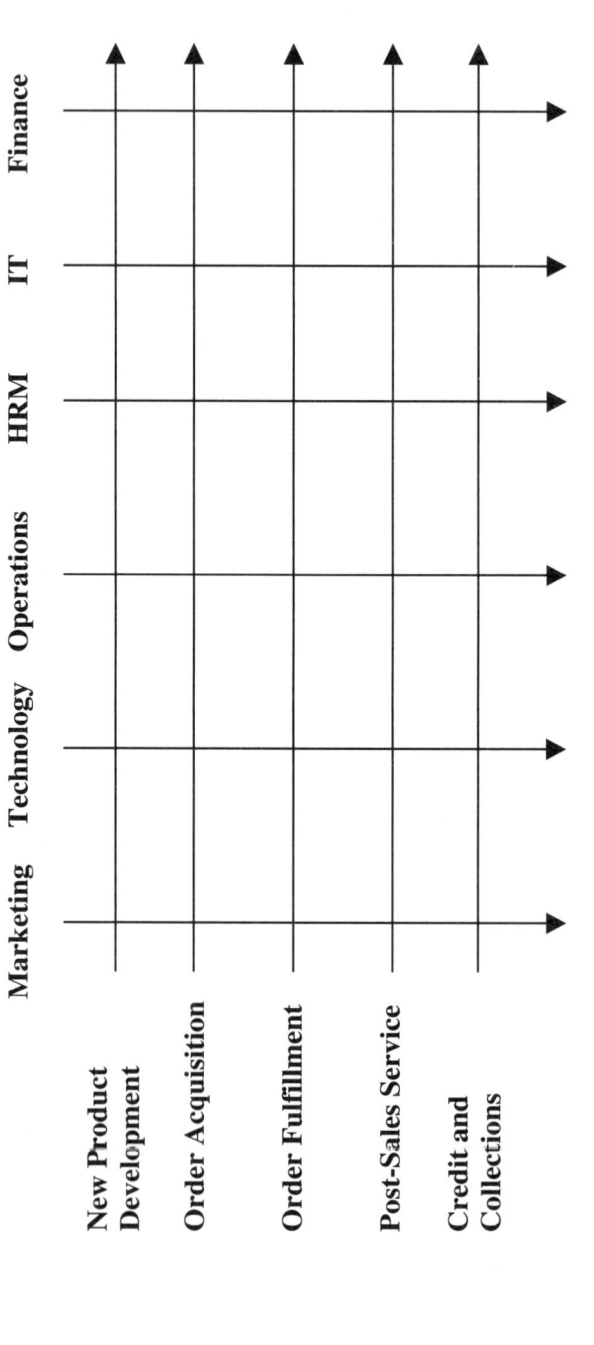

	Marketing	Technology	Operations	HRM	IT	Finance
New Product Development						
Order Acquisition						
Order Fulfillment						
Post-Sales Service						
Credit and Collections						

both individually and as an integrated set to get the work done, meet customer expectations, and to do so at a competitive advantage. While you should feel free to substitute your own process names, we recommend that you restrict your list to the business processes that are ultimately visible to your customers.

The outcomes of each of these business processes are visible to the customer. Therefore, if we judge them the same way that the customer does, while adding in our own measures of productivity, we will know whether or not more alignment is necessary. These days, when many customers are powerful and have choices, we can expect the voice of the customer to help, in part, with this assessment. But the customer cannot tell us how to fix broken processes because much of their content is invisible to them. It is up to us to understand how cross-functional work—as indicated in Figure 2-2 by horizontal process arrows—gets done. This means that we need to think "horizontally" across the traditional business functions, where necessary know-how and other resources flow together to serve the customer as value is added.

Together, business functions and business processes constitute a company's operating system, which can also be considered its strategy-in-use if you adopt the commonsense view of strategy as what you do to get what you want. The AA model lets us share knowledge about customers and the effectiveness and efficiency of every function with every business process, thus revealing its real strategy rather than its intended strategy.

The AA model offers a new picture of a business that will help you and your staff execute your plan. This framework is simple and firmly anchored in reality. It is easy to use, and stimulates fresh questions and eagerness for action. It attracts attention to the problems of making the operating system customer-centered; working at maximum speed, reliability, and productivity; and delivering heightened earnings.

By using it, you will develop a concrete, more complete sense of how successfully you are meeting the needs of current customers, even as you take steps to attract future ones. The alignment frame should help you to sharpen your judgment and to sift out the nuggets from the endless ongoing flow of information impacting you day by day. It should help you work faster than before, avoid customer traps, and enhance your ability to define your own future.

For today's tightly interconnected supply chains, this new way of thinking about a business can help a management team reconceptualize its situation in an administratively neutral context, seeing the performance drivers more precisely and alerting them to the identity of critical issues that afflict them all. Using the AA model as a platform for gathering information, and then converting it to knowledge through collective assessment, will sensitize their listening. This method will help them to act as enterprise leaders who are able to coordinate their activities with each other and, as necessary, with others who work in their suppliers' and channel organizations. Alignment yields dramatic benefits for both customers and company alike.

Aligned Operations Make a Business Customer-Centered

While working with companies, we observed that once people mastered the AA model, we were able to stand aside since they immediately began asking new questions—often about long-festering problems. For example, they asked, "How well organized are we to serve our customers?" "Where do we get in our own way?" "Where are our efforts poorly aligned and leaving us working at cross-purposes?" "How well do our operations reflect our stated strategy?" "How effectively does our strategy shape operations?" "How does our overall operating system—rather than just our operations management function—constrain our success or impede our strategic flexibility?"

The customer, appropriately, receives massive attention from those who apply the AA model, since it promotes enterprise-wide thinking about problems in meeting customer needs and how to remedy them. Many misalignments can be repaired quite quickly and easily once the managers involved recognize the importance of customer-centering to the company's business processes—that is, when they work together to align action across every business process to serve the company's customers.

Once management has gained a shared sense of its misalignments, and agrees that they are worth addressing, the next step toward becoming a customer-centered organization is for management to measure process performance in light of the customer's expectations rather than with measures that have only internal significance. Over time, organizations that work to achieve this external measure of success will be better positioned to outperform those that focus on internal measures and stress cost control. Remember, ever since W. Edwards Deming first got our attention, we have realized that if you do not measure it, you do not manage it. Hence, use the AA model to focus your team's energy where it counts, on the customer's measure of success.

There are also other, more subtle but significant advantages that the AA model offers. The clear picture afforded by the AA model's network of functions and processes can also become the foundation of a shared language that managers need to work together, to identify the problems affecting the enterprise, and to align their actions with the corporate purpose. This model of the business puts the operating system at the center of strategy where it belongs. Moreover, because the abstracted AA model representation of the organization can usually be presented on one page or one overhead slide, it can be grasped easily and then discussed in its entirety. It allows teams to explore where they are meeting their responsibilities with respect to other elements of the organization, think freshly about their situations, change their positions, and deal with their successes and shortcomings on an administratively neutral stage. The holistic view afforded by the AA model helps them to meet their delegated responsibilities and to address the alignment problems of their corporate organizational units without compromising the enterprise.

Using the AA model to size up an organization has also proven helpful to executives who want a grounded assessment of how the company is doing. You can acquire far richer feedback than only top-line sales and bottom-line profitability when reviewing the results from a series of consecutive operating cycles. As information flows in and out, customer relationships are either enhanced or damaged. Similarly, every business process demonstrates its current capabilities and, since practice makes perfect, management has the opportunity to expand and improve those capabilities, eliminating gaps where better alignment is both possible and meaningful in its impact on the customer. The terms *capabilities* and *capability gaps* need to be carefully understood and used consistently by all who participate in your action alignment exercise.

▲ *Capabilities* are measures of the performance of business processes along dimensions defined by the customer's needs and expectations, such as time, cost, quality, functionality, flexibility, and acuity. The market test of a capability is whether it satisfies the company's target customers. The competitive test is whether those customers judge the company to be advantaged, compared to its rivals on that dimension, and positioned to be their preferred supplier.

▲ *Capability gaps* must be judged relative to the competition. A gap indicates a failure to deliver better than the competition, on some dimension, what the customers want. Time matters when assessing the strategic significance of a gap and the urgency of repairing it.

Note that since we have defined process capabilities in terms that matter most to customers, there can be no single all-purpose list of capabilities for every company to try to achieve. Figure 2-3, therefore, is simply illustrative. We include it here so that you can begin to think about the ways in which your company ought to think about the performance of your various business processes.

Figure 2-3. Some measures of process capability.

Business Process	Capability Indicator	Company
New Product Development	• Product introduction cycle time • Technological innovation • Product functionality	Hewlett-Packard
Order Acquisition	• Web site ease-of-use • Accuracy of delivery promises	Amazon.com
Order Fulfillment	• % accuracy in order delivery (item, quantity, date) • Cost per delivered case	Colgate-Palmolive
Post-Sales Service	• Quality of maintenance/ repairs • Service convenience/ accessibility	Lexus
Credit and Collections	• Accuracy of bills issued • Accuracy of payments credited	MCI Worldcom

Shared Knowledge Using the AA Model

Now, using the grid of the AA model along with a good sense of what process capabilities are to anchor our thinking, we will outline a proven approach for gathering relevant strategic knowledge from across a single business. The purpose of gathering this knowledge is to share it, and to trigger planning and action. This special kind of operational audit is best completed by a team of executives who represent the business's various functions and processes.

As knowledge is gathered and organized, management often recognizes misalignments that can be repaired to significantly improve business performance. For example, they may decide to strengthen their management of functional/process interactions and to eliminate significant misalignments and useless conflict. Next, they are likely to identify opportunities to improve day-to-day operating performance at the enterprise level. The whole process, which is outlined in Figure 2-4, sets the stage for subsequent planning. It is analogous to an athlete's having a checkup before getting into shape to take on new challenges.

Figure 2-4. Enterprise facts: effectiveness and efficiency through alignment.

1. Assess the importance of each business function in contributing to the success of each business process.
2. Identify the core functions and the core business processes.
3. Assess the degree of alignment and misalignment across functions and processes.
4. Check the short-term results, including the enterprise's competitive advantage, the customer satisfaction it delivers, and how its partners' performance impacts its own performance.
5. Determine process capabilities and capability gaps.

The first item in Figure 2-4 refers to facts that management should already know. As you use the AA model as an organizing frame, you need to catalog the facts and focus on each node or intersection of a process and function by asking: Is this interaction important to the performance of the enterprise? How important, and why? Should we highlight this relationship and spend time discussing its implications?

We have found this first step is rather easy to complete and, since all business processes are cross-functional, we recommend making the debate cross-functional too, by including representatives from every function. If teams from each business process are also involved, their members will quickly appreciate that different points of view exist across the organization. Some may be the causes of dysfunctional delay, neglect, and confusion. Having cross-functional membership on the audit team ensures there is a focus on process objectives and limited functional bias. Note that this first step will be facilitated by familiarity with business activities, flows, and interactions at the process level. A business unit that has already redesigned several business processes should be able to provide an accurate picture quite readily. Others may have to map how their business processes actually work.

Your current functional and process management teams should collectively decide what matters most and show how their views about performance match those of customers. Use the AA model as a framework to concentrate your attention on the most significant nodes where functions have their greatest impact on the processes, either by making their planned contributions or by impeding the company's efforts to serve its customers.

As an example of how to modify the standard audit templates to reflect what actually happens, consider the dynamic and highly competitive hotel industry. When performing an audit of companies in that industry, we suggest collapsing the order fulfillment and post-sales service processes into one combined or "entwined" core business process. After all, aside from a relatively minor commitment to handling complaints from dissatisfied customers sometime after completing their stay at the hotel, the bulk of post-sales service for a hotel occurs at the hotel itself in face-to-face interactions between customers and employees. This is exactly what we mean by order fulfillment in this industry: Every "moment of truth," from the time that the customer arrives to register until he or she checks out and leaves the premises, is a post-sales service test.

Although this may appear to be a rather straightforward observation that could be applied to almost any service-sector business, you should introduce it at an early stage of the action alignment exercise to seek its implications. That way you can persuasively argue for any needed changes in alignment between the company's various business functions and this core process. We found that many issues, including organizational structure, staffing, information systems, and performance measurement, needed to be resolved to improve fit and flow in the specific hotel enterprises we studied. Without such process-centered thinking, guests could easily be stranded with no one ready to respond to their needs.

Identify Core Functions and Core Business Processes

Experience shows that the audit team will find the core function and process identities quite clear from answering the question: What nodes matter most? They are the functions and processes that have the greatest direct impact on enterprise success in the customer's eyes. Core processes make the greatest contribution to building the enterprise's competitive advantage and success in the marketplace. Core capabilities distinguish the firm from its rivals and bind it to its customers. Further leverage of a core process is likely to enhance enterprise performance.

Consider the one-page graph shown in Figure 2-5, which highlights Dell's core function: operations, and its core process: order fulfillment. The original purpose of this drawing was to help another management team understand Dell. The core elements are drawn with bold lines to focus management's attention on a high-impact issue, and key objectives are listed below (function) and to the right of the alignment grid (process). Service is becoming increasingly more important—hence, the rings linking the fulfillment and service processes. Dell has set the industry standard for fast delivery of high-quality personal computers that are made to order and can be shipped overnight or in two business days direct to the customer. The customer expects convenience, low price, the latest technology, and delivery as promised.

In Dell's business model, there are a few factors that are very important. For most customers, the first factor is access to the company for information and to place orders. The next factor is the company's capability to quickly build high-quality, state-of-the-art PC systems at a low price from available, defect-free components, and to provide immediate pickup and delivery. Finally, there is the company's ability to handle all post-sales questions. Meeting these customer needs requires a fully integrated supply chain, a commitment that has implications for IT, job definitions, and supplier and distribution partnerships.

Note that the team anticipated Dell would strengthen its information connections between the order acquisition and order fulfillment processes and post-sales service. During this study, the connection between order acquisition and order fulfillment within Dell was assessed as a strength, while the connection between order fulfillment and post-sales service seemed to need strengthening to ensure that every customer query could be handled in a

Figure 2-5. The AA model of Dell.

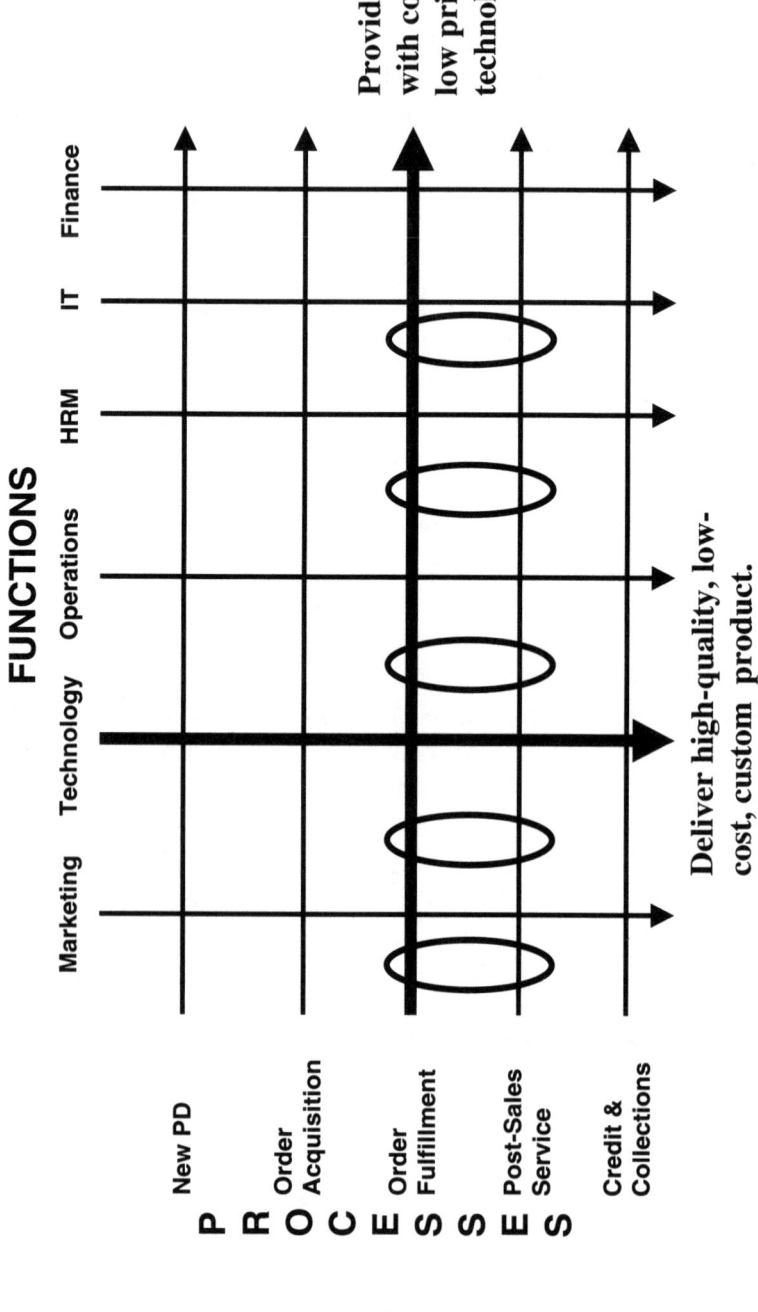

FUNCTIONS

	Marketing	Technology	Operations	HRM	IT	Finance

P New PD

R Order
O Acquisition

C Order
E Fulfillment
S

S Post-Sales
E Service
S

Credit &
Collections

Provide customer with convenience, low price, and latest technology.

Deliver high-quality, low-cost, custom product.

seamless manner. In this study, management's attention was attracted to this prospective change in the competitive situation by the rings linking the two processes. Also worth noting is that a superb order fulfillment process eliminates many service requests, such as tracking orders, dealing with incomplete or incorrect PC configurations that were delivered, or dealing with in-use performance failures.

Now that you have a feeling for the first two steps in applying the AA model, let us look more closely at how it can be used as a device to help you share critical knowledge and to choose priority action initiatives. First, before proceeding with any self-study, your management team, in the interests of efficiency, may choose to exclude some functions from deeper investigation due to their minimal direct impacts on enterprise success. Less common, but possible, is a decision to eliminate one or more of the business processes from further investigation at this juncture. For example, you might do so when it is clear that one process is in fact *the* problem.

Here, the important issue is the team's confidence in the legitimacy of their work, so avoid working on "problems" that either do not exist or that are relatively minor in consequence. Note, too, that to maximize the meaningfulness of the work, we recommend restricting the study to the customer-visible or customer-focused business processes only, rather than reviewing all the logistical and resourcing support or culture-building processes that may exist in a company. This is because misalignments on these processes can directly injure the company in its customers' eyes. They are strategic. This second step is complete, therefore, when every "critical node" has been identified.

Assess Alignments and Misalignments

Alignment across functions and processes exists when every process has timely access to the specific functional expertise and resources it requires. For example, in the white goods industry, marketing staff routinely provide timely and accurate information on customers' requirements for new home appliances to the concept development stage of the new product development process. Assessing the marketing staff's contributions to new product development encompasses other potential competencies too, such as testing the acceptance of a new product prototype or conducting smooth product launches.

Alignment along any cross-functional business process is achieved through a combination of attributes: responsiveness; information sharing; decision-making speed and focus; adequate and timely resourcing; timely contributions to problem solving; and conflict resolution. Of course, customer satisfaction with every business process is the ultimate sign of an aligned organization, but responsiveness and these other internal attributes of alignment are at the roots of satisfaction. Thus, these are the dimensions along which you and your team needs to share knowledge and then trigger improvements. Later, customers will see improved process capabilities as a result of your focus on these *hidden* dimensions of the process.

Similar to the manner in which we identified core processes in Figure 2-5, Figure 2-6 identifies and catalogs misalignments by calling attention to problem nodes, which you will recall are the critical points at which information is transferred in any communication network. In the AA model, nodes are the points of interaction, where a business function needs to provide a business process manager with what he or she needs to succeed for both the customers and the company. You can share knowledge on the current status and ultimate importance of the various nodes by having all managers who have responsibilities for these activities catalog where they believe there are problems or opportunities for performance improvements and where competitive advantage could be enhanced. The

Figure 2-6. Alignment/misalignment of functional competencies and process capabilities.

Poor Alignment between Marketing & New Product Development

FUNCTIONS

Not Enough Project Leaders

Poor Alignment
- Earnings pressure & reporting at odds with R&D need

Capabilities (Gaps)
- Inefficient
- No core capabilities

Functions (columns): Marketing, Technology, Operations, HRM, IT, Finance

PROCESSES (rows):
- New Product Development
- Order Acquisition
- Order Fulfillment
- Post-Sales Service
- Credit & Collections

- Few markets
- Poor logistics

Poor Linkage/Alignment between Operations and Fulfillment
- Strikes
- Long breaks
- Resistant to change

(In)competencies
- Limited skill set
- No core competencies

No Linkage between Quality Improvement and Operations
- Inefficient production
- Long design → product

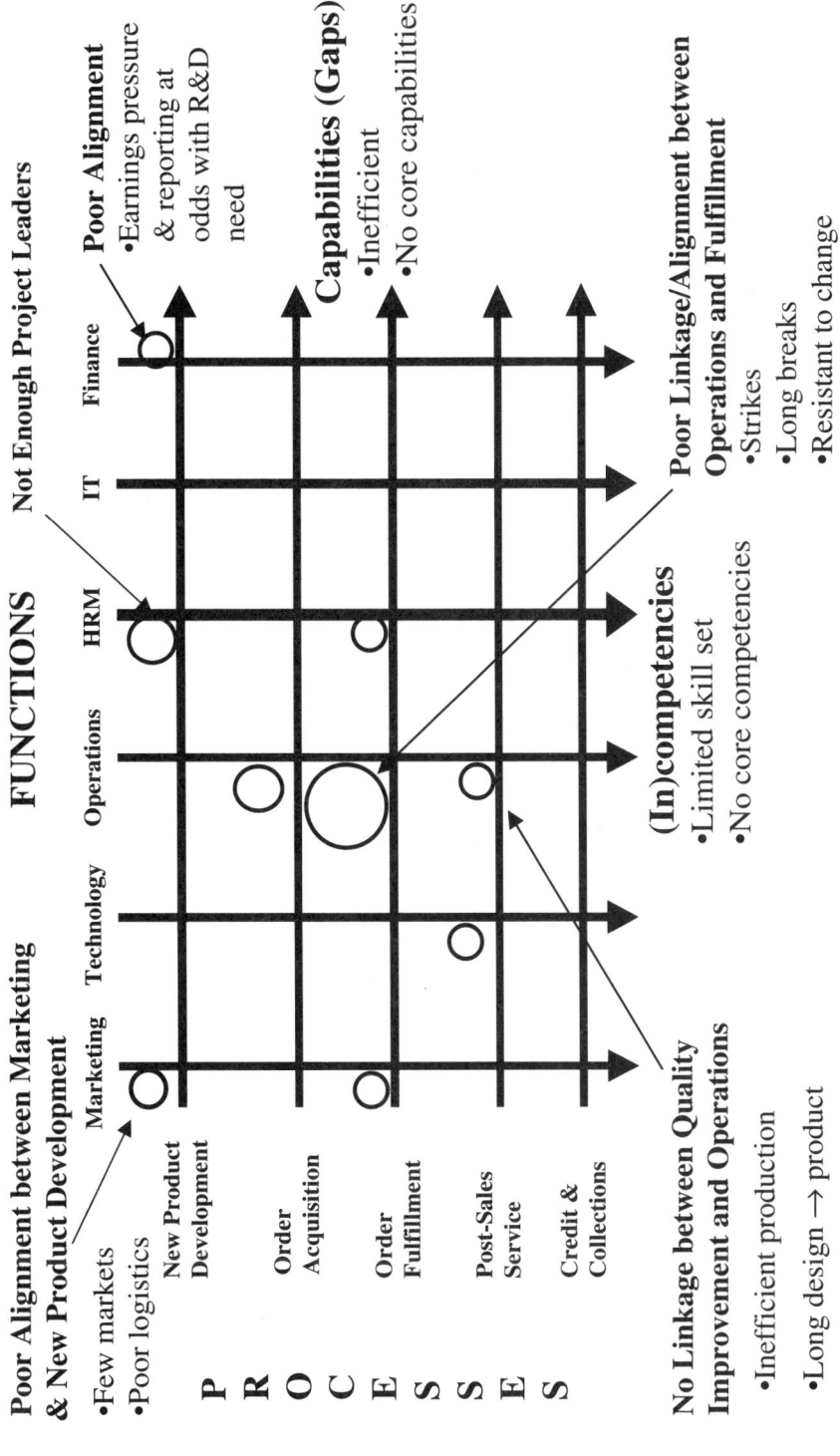

point of this knowledge-sharing exercise is to identify critical misalignments at these nodal points of interaction.

For example, consider some of the results of an audit of a manufacturer of prototype and custom-designed high-pressure and temperature control equipment for industrial, food, pharmaceutical, and cosmetics companies. At one time, the company was under cost pressure in its traditional markets, and management was evaluating strategies to exploit a technological breakthrough that had the potential to allow them to migrate downstream. Their plan was to break into two new markets, one serving the franchise fast-food industry and the other serving the traditional domestic home-cooking market—a move that would take it closer to the consumer than ever before.

Because the study team believed that there were misalignments between customer needs and action along every business process, it highlighted them with small circles that are offset slightly from the relevant functional process nodes, as illustrated in Figure 2-6. The greater the misalignment that occurred, the bigger the circle. They also noticed that this publicly held firm was under earnings pressure even as it considered stepping up its research and development (R and D)—hence, the circles under finance and on the new product development process arrow. There was also a dearth of experienced new product development project leaders—a critical shortcoming that shows at the new product development and HRM node (see the relatively large circle on the new product development arrow under the HRM function). Moreover, they realized the company lacked the process capabilities needed to fulfill orders in its currently unserved market. Indeed, this last capability gap was large, as represented by the large circle under operations on the fulfillment process arrow.

This last figure schematically portrays key results for the managers who are participating on this AA model audit team. Their results then become a platform for debate and planning. Circle by circle, it highlights problems that management needs to overcome to realize the full potential of its long-established manufacturing business before venturing into new markets. The method is straightforward: Question what is going on function by function, process by process, and node by node, and then note the results achieved. Establish the facts first, then try to define likely causes for your results, whether they be good or bad. Next, test whether the suspected causes hold up under review or need closer definition or more investigation. Then decide on a course of action. This process will quickly move your team toward action—much like Jack Welch's *Work Out* at GE—but the result is better performance in the customer's eyes.

There are some additional tests that you and the rest of your audit team may find useful once you identify the most significant misalignments:

▲ *To what extent does the specific misalignment experienced at a particular node interfere with the company's ability to meet its customers' expectations and build its competitive advantages?*

▲ *What will it take to fix the problem?* A solution means developing an alignment strategy and assessing its costs in terms such as information and skill enhancement and behavioral incentives.

▲ *At present, is management technically, functionally, and administratively competent to do the job?* If they are inadequate to the task, an alternative path may be the best approach. Sometimes, outside resources can be brought in to develop a solution. But the use of outsiders here brings two risks: first, that the organization will become dependent on its consultants, and, second, that the outsiders will bring their canned solutions to the table rather than addressing the real needs of the organization. In this last case, the consultants may merely shift the burden of the misalignment to another node.

To address these questions and diagnose causes, you should again insist on cataloging the facts and having the study team evidence its conclusions in a straightforward way, for example, by assessing every function's contribution to a particular business process's performance during a reasonable time frame prior to the study. Gaps in such evidence can be filled in subjectively if there is a reasonable consensus among the individuals involved, or by targeted studies, should there be important unresolved conflict with respect to one or more functions or processes. For example, customers might be surveyed to ascertain whether management has a realistic perception of customer-focused performance across the enterprise—that is, whether it knows the facts or simply thinks it does.

Check Short-Term Results

Your next step in the AA-model audit is to check the recent results of your business processes. Consider any available indicators of your competitive advantage and customer satisfaction and how the performance of your supplier or channel impacts your own. Be careful here, because how and what you measure influences what you see and is likely to shape your plan of action. For example, there are several ways to measure market share for an allergy drug: share of prescriptions, share of prescribing physicians, share of teaching hospitals, or share of sufferers. Each measure of market share gives special insights into the causes of the drug company's frustrations, difficulties, and successes.

Check your results against several benchmarks:

▲ *Results vs. Objectives*—Are you achieving your objectives and executing your intended strategy? Should either strategy or objectives be changed?
▲ *Results vs. Best Practice*—Are you close to achieving ideal performance vis-à-vis the global best of the class?
▲ *Results vs. the Past*—Are you improving at an acceptable rate?
▲ *Results vs. Competition*—Where do we have competitive advantage, and where are we at a disadvantage?
▲ *Our Supplier's Results vs. Their Competitors' Results* and the impact of this situation on our own. Are our problems caused by the company we keep? Or do we owe our success to their efforts?

We have found these five comparisons, as a set, useful for reviewing performance, helping managers to define new objectives and to discover new performance measures, defining realistic and competitive performance goals, and in selecting priorities for resource allocation. Clearly, each of these potential comparative measures requires data. Sometimes, however, informed opinions have to suffice. The point is to create the best knowledge base you can by sharing the various indications that you have about your short-term results.

We have also observed that when you evaluate results, what you see depends on when you look, just as how you measure partly determines what you see. Sometimes, a company in transition from one strategy to another may suffer falling profits even as it gathers new strength. The United States brewing industry has gone through several periods during which profitability was proven to be a poor indicator of shifting competitiveness. During the 1970s and 1980s, for example, the largest brewers reported modest profits. In fact, their operating strategies were highly advantaged vis-à-vis the regional brewers who were their competitors on a market-by-market basis. This competitive advantage was used to fund aggressive marketing but, in the short run, the annual profits reported by companies such as Anheuser-Busch fell, even as they increased their market share.

Determine Process Capabilities and Capability Gaps

Now, focus on your present process capabilities while remembering that process redesign has both short- and long-term consequences. Done correctly, redesign yields horizontal (that is, cross-functional) processes aimed at serving particular customers in ways that result in short-term business success. Whether or not these same processes promote longer-term competitive advantage depends on the specific capabilities they exhibit and on performance improvements: Are they valued by the customer, easily achieved by others, improvable, and adaptable to new demand patterns? Identify, for each core business process, your capabilities and capability gaps given the strategy in use and the customers being served.

The goal of the action alignment process is to identify major sources of waste, while the locus of capability gaps highlights avenues for improvement and determines the investments needed to both satisfy your customers more completely and to bolster your competitive position. These outputs constitute the basis for highly targeted performance improvement plans. For example, the study will uncover constraints, bottlenecks, and the identity of the forces blocking change, whether they are due to lack of shared vision, incentives, or capacity; political opposition; or some implementation problem, especially when they impact the company's core process or core competence. Subsequent planning should record how management intends to address these problems and multiply the enterprise's success both horizontally and vertically, that is, by process and by function. The planning should address levering the company's competitively advantaged capabilities and investments in new capabilities to eliminate gaps, thereby enhancing the competitiveness of the enterprise.

Achieve Dynamic Alignment

By applying the AA model, management can be challenged to share what it knows and, then, to carefully reassess its current customers' needs and performance expectations before moving on to fix specific "problems." Members of the management team should ask themselves, How well can we serve these customers in the near future with the capabilities we already have? Next, they can turn to a more macro analysis, and attempt to justify their own focused process objectives against the unfolding competitive, technological, and societal situations that define the emerging environment of the enterprise. This type of approach can raise fundamental questions about changes in the current market and the future demand for the company's products and services.

The issue is one of balance. Here are some more questions to help you stay focused: Can the capability platform adequately serve the current customer base, given its emerging needs and performance expectations? Or is it out of balance, forcing you to face the costs of your capability gaps? Is the effort that the business can muster in balance with the demands of the market—that is, does it have the capabilities to win? Is the plan feasible? Are there resources and capacity available to do even more?

Alignment is simple in concept but difficult to achieve. One problem impeding alignment is that managers often lack a good way of thinking and talking about alignment and the roles of the business functions. The AA model should help overcome this communication barrier. Another problem is that alignment can be frustratingly difficult to sustain because the working units of any organization can drift apart quite easily as its managers become distracted by new opportunities, or even problems of their own making. Here are some pointers to keep in mind:

▲ To maintain alignment, always know your customers, their expectations, and how their expectations are changing. This is no mean feat in itself, but you are probably already aware of techniques for gathering this critical knowledge.

▲ Verify that your strategy is aligned with the needs of the real market. Are the core elements of your strategy still important to your customers? Sometimes every commitment is competitively relevant but, if untested and unquestioned, some strategic commitments may be out-of-date and may actually accelerate the company's drift into obsolescence.

▲ Keep every business process customer-centered. Once we have a good sense of customer expectations and have verified that our core elements are on target, we can make a hard choice: either organize to deliver what they want or, alternatively, exit the market.

▲ Deal with the whole business. In most companies, the efforts that TQM and reengineering stimulate are restricted to one or two business processes, with many business functions sitting smugly on the sidelines unaffected. The action alignment study we have described should help your organization get all business processes moving in the right direction.

Charts and frameworks such as the AA model are intended to help by provoking questions that contribute to the agenda for an administratively neutral forum where the causes of problems can be assessed and where opportunities to improve performance can be crafted. To avoid the trap of trying to do everything at once but accomplishing nothing, we advise insisting on strategic relevance, improvement feasibility, and cost as the criteria for selecting which misalignments to work on.

Conclusion

There is a heightened need for enterprise-wide alignment in the knowledge economy. It is a necessary response to the growing complexity of our business world, and, when focused on customer satisfaction, its achievement is easy to recognize. Companies that have achieved full customer satisfaction are known for their ability to execute their strategy and fulfill orders. In the personal computer industry, Dell has been well aligned for several years, while Compaq and IBM, early on, suffered the costs of misalignment, one notable outcome being the exceptional growth of Dell itself.

The ultimate reason for alignment, however, is that aligned action multiplies the force that any one organizational unit can deliver to its customers by levering the resources of the whole organization. Effective organizations concentrate their forces on the market and deploy their energy with good timing, in terms of both speed and actions taken. Speed and the accumulated effect of a series of reinforcing actions combine to deliver even greater impact than they might have achieved singly.

This chapter presented the AA model, an approach for sharing knowledge as you "size up" your organization to establish how customer-centered you are at present and what gaps should be closed to improve that situation. Following this approach, an important first step toward becoming a knowing corporation is to promote the kind of customer-centered thinking that will prepare your management team to work cross-functionally and to focus their minds on determining how to win in your current marketplace. It provides the opportunity for a management team to share key knowledge and to know where it really stands.

Knowing how customer-centered you are is a prerequisite for strengthening your position in your current market. The alignment that you achieve based on sharing such knowledge also supports strategies for stretching into new markets and toward new opportunities. But, first, you need to know how to serve your current customers better and more profitably by doing less. In the next chapter, we offer an approach for sharing the knowledge that will help you to make these critical decisions.

Notes

1. David Garvin, "Leveraging Processes for Strategic Advantage," *Harvard Business Review*, September/October 1995, p. 88.
2. Earlier, we called this the "enterprise model" and described it in similar terms in Kenneth J. Hatten and Stephen R. Rosenthal, "Managing the Process-Centered Enterprise," *Long Range Planning*, 32:3, June 1999, pp. 293–310.

3
Checking Feasibility: Customers, Capabilities, and Competencies

The full cost of customer-centering is higher than you might initially imagine. First, you must consider the impacts of rising customer expectations. Then, there is the cost of world-class capacity. Finally, there is the cost of making it happen. Whatever your business is, achieving excellence in your customers' eyes will require many distinct competencies and intense cooperation among those who must play a part in dealing with customers and satisfying their needs.

As both costs and the complexity of customer-centering proliferate, your company is likely to have many incentives to join with others to form networked enterprises. We use the term *enterprise* to refer to a linked set of companies that, together, serve a market segment through a contracted or partnered set of business relationships. The new competitive reality is that enterprise profitability is a prerequisite, over the long term, for corporate profitability. Hence, the networked enterprises that your company participates in, and in particular, those that you lead, will determine its success and your shareholders' returns. And you may well be called upon to negotiate these deals and to manage the relationships that they establish.

To meet this need, this chapter offers an efficient approach that shortcuts the task of assessing the fit of any business with its customers. An appropriate assessment can be completed without the full systems mapping that you mastered in Chapter 2 to help you to bring your own operations to maximum customer satisfaction and efficiency. Now you will master a similar process for getting your own and your partners' people up on the balcony to view, from the outside, how well your customers are being served by the multiorganization enterprise of which you are a part. To accomplish this, you will need a solid sense of your own company, its partners, its customers, and its competitors. Then you will be able to make the right decisions about knowledge-sharing on a day-to-day basis. After you have mastered the new process introduced in this chapter, you will be able to not only lift your own operations to new levels of performance but will also gain an awareness of the factors critical for creating and managing an advantaged networked enterprise.

The Power of Enterprise Leadership

Let us begin by appreciating the power of the enterprise view. You are probably aware of the new IT systems designed for enterprise management that facilitate networking, contracting, and partnering for various business processes. These systems have the promise of affording many people full and simultaneous access to information, while creating opportunities for corporate-wide learning. The latest technologies, including the Internet, have also drastically reduced the costs of coordination across, as well as within, organizational boundaries. They enable the design of networked multicompany product and service delivery systems that are capable of higher quality, faster response, and lower total cost than would otherwise be possible. Soon customers will know you by the company you keep.

The power of enterprise management, then, is that you can improve customer satisfaction by networking with other organizations that will do some of the work. In other words, you can do less in-house and lower your costs while executing better for the customer. But all of your enterprise relationships have to be made with care. Linking the capabilities and competencies of several organizations into a single, integrated, customer-centered enterprise calls for the kind of knowledge-sharing that also brings risk. Care is needed to promote the enterprise while you protect your own competencies and distinctiveness—your ability to stay in business and adapt to change.

The basic business strategy here is: Work your comparative advantages—do more of what you do especially well—by using your capital and management assets more effectively while creating a stronger competitive position for the whole enterprise by drawing on the strengths of others. When you know what you do best, you can then tap what others do best, often discovering that it can be both better and cheaper to work with them rather than doing it yourself. Then you can focus on enterprise leadership, that is, positioning your company as the architect of a network of companies that you coordinate to serve a targeted set of customers from a more advantaged position. You will have created a way to deliver products and services at greater advantage but with reduced asset commitments.

Doing better by doing less requires specialized knowledge to contract out some activities, and to find and manage the enterprise partners who will do other segments of the value-added work. This may allow you to exit from entire business processes in which you either have no competitive edge or your value-added is low. To identify appropriate opportunities of this kind, you have to know yourself well and know how to size up other corporations' strengths. Furthermore, while vision at the top may define targets for enterprise opportunity, implementing the vision will call for some new competencies of your own. Some operating executives will become responsible for negotiating the partnerships or supply contracts. They will select the risks to be taken and have the responsibility of developing an in-house team of people who can function inside and outside their own organization to make the whole thing work.

Defining Organizational Competencies

We have found that most managers are considerably more comfortable thinking about the capabilities of their business processes than about the knowledge required to successfully create those processes. So now, let us formally define the term *organizational competency*, and then explain why competencies matter and why they are the foundations of your own competitiveness:

- ▲ Competencies are the cognitive characteristics of an organization, its know-how, and are typically the responsibility of business functions. The organization gains competitive power when its competencies are marshaled through cross-functional process design and levered with materials, labor, and capital to deliver customer satisfaction.
- ▲ Competency gaps, or inadequacies, are critical shortcomings in organizational know-how, where the company is behind the state-of-the-art in a particular function. They are significant because the customer-visible business processes are cross-

functional and, regardless of their design, process performance ultimately rests on the knowledge available to the company and how well it is applied. Competency gaps and inadequacies thwart intent.

To understand organizational competencies, think of them as collective expertise, conceptually distinct from the process capabilities that are seen by the customer. The most familiar competencies are those that directly relate to the objectives of traditional business functions, as illustrated in Figure 3-1. You have probably seen the term *core competency* used to refer to expertise in some specific research and development arena. Here, however, competency is a broader concept that encompasses the full set of business functions because functional competencies are the roots of competitive advantage. Knowing your own, your partners', your customers' (when they are businesses), and your competitors' competencies is crucial to forging a competitive enterprise and protecting your own. This is why "sharing" among corporations is a code word for both sharing and deliberately protecting some of your competencies as a matter of survival. Sharing demands self-interested discrimination when you have partners and competitors. Strategizing at the enterprise level, and executing enterprise-level strategies, requires that every manager is aware of the role of knowledge in your corporate and business strategies. Only then can he or she tilt the world in your favor by optimizing the use of your own scarce resources, even as you benefit from the strengths of your contractors and partners.

Seeking 3C Balance

By adding the concept of organizational competency to that of process capability, managers can think more readily about strategy and their alignment with target customers.

Figure 3-1. Functional competencies and companies that have them.

Marketing	Brand management for diversifying into new multimedia businesses	*Disney*
	Monitoring customer satisfaction	*Solectron*
	Demand creation	*Nike*
	Direct custom marketing (sales)	*Dell/Micron*
Technology	Mechanical design for precision paper movement equipment	*Xerox*
	State-of-the-art design of microprocessor chip families	*Intel*
	Design of new standards for lifelike sound reproduction	*Bose*
	Product design for high-volume assembly	*Gillette*
	Industrial design	*Sony*
Operations	Integrated global logistics	*FedEx*
	Purchasing	*P & G*
HR	State-of-the-art training in a corporate university	*Motorola*
	Recruiting, hiring, training, and retaining part-time labor	*McDonalds*
	Managing personnel recruitment and separations	*McKinsey* *Arthur Andersen*
Finance	Raising debt capital at rate better than competition	*JP Morgan*
IT	Using IT creatively to change cost structures in multiple-business processes	*Cisco*

Collectively, the company's customers, capabilities, and competencies can be used to represent its current strategy and competitive positioning. Therefore, by weighing the advantages of your competencies and capabilities against the constraints of your capability and competency gaps, you can make a summarized assessment of where you stand vis-à-vis your customers and, by comparison, where your competitors stand with respect to their customers and yours. Remember that competencies, as we have defined the term here, support your capabilities, and that your capabilities should be geared toward presenting a high-performing face to your customers while delivering satisfaction to them and an advantage to you.

For convenience, we will refer to *customers, capabilities,* and *competencies* as the 3Cs. Figure 3-2 may help you to develop an intuitive feel for the concept of 3C balance. Here we have represented the 3Cs as the points of a triangle. After identifying your 3C status by sharing knowledge across your company and comparing it to your competitor's, you will be able to address this key question: Do we have the functional competencies and process capabilities to serve our target customers at a competitive advantage? Do the 3Cs fit together?

By focusing the minds of your team members on your

Figure 3-2. The 3Cs.

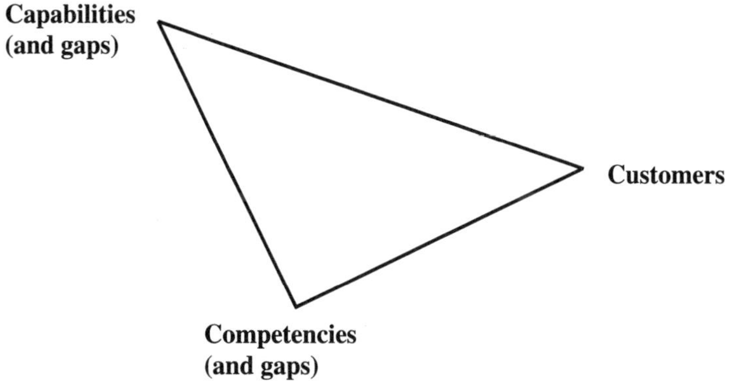

Capabilities (and gaps)

Customers

Competencies (and gaps)

customers' needs and expectations—for example, by asking how they judge your organization's performance—they will quickly appreciate where you have an edge and why. Similarly, they will also see where an edge is lacking, making the triangle unbalanced, and how contracting or partnering could be useful.

Now, to illustrate what we mean by "fit among the 3Cs," we will focus on a singularly successful company, the Cleveland-based Lincoln Electric Company, which is the world's leading maker of welding equipment. Later, we will use another company as an example of how a networked enterprise was created by harnessing the resources of several different businesses to serve a single target market.

Understanding the Lincoln Electric Example

Since well before World War II, Lincoln Electric has been a manufacturing company with a product line restricted to welding equipment, welding consumables, and small electric motors. John Lincoln, one of the company's two founders, was an inventor who recognized early that welding was a huge opportunity. He saw it as an alternative market for the motor-generator sets that he and his brother were already producing for electric automobiles.

In 1941, Lincoln Electric, by then the clear leader in its industry, responded to a request from the United States government for more industry capacity for the war effort by observing that there was plenty of capacity—it was simply being used inefficiently. The Lincoln brothers then opened all of their proprietary technology, methods, and equipment designs to other companies. As a result, by the end of the war, Lincoln and its competitors all essentially employed the same production capability and enjoyed similar costs. But Lincoln quickly changed that situation. Within six months of the war's end, Lincoln's productivity per worker, at three times the industry norm, had once again outpaced its competitors.

Lincoln Electric's customer base was wide, ranging from small shops with hand welders, whose ratio of machine cost to consumables was 7:1, to large steel-bridge fabricators and shipyards, with a 1:7 ratio of machine cost to consumables. In 1947, Lincoln's strategy was "to give its customers more and more of a better product at a lower and lower price." This formidable recipe for success at Lincoln was continuously employed for decades.

What made it possible for Lincoln to so quickly gain the upper hand and force companies like GE out of the welding industry? In 3C language, the answer lies in its many complementary competencies that were buttressed by supporting administrative systems and long-honored contracts between the company and all its employees, white- and blue-collar alike. Lincoln is nonunionized and well-known for paying its workers on piece rates. However, Lincoln also guarantees its people a base salary for thirty hours of work each week, after two years of employment. To allow the company to honor this policy, Lincoln had to intentionally constrain its growth while maintaining its 3C balance.

Lincoln is a customer-centered company. Although it does little formal R and D, it is the technology leader because it has mastered the source of new ideas—ideas that are learned in action during its consultations with customers about their problems. Lincoln Electric has made specific relationships with its trusted customers and marshaled key resources to support future growth.

Lincoln knows that competence leads to capabilities—the ability to do things—especially when a reliable customer relationship can be leveraged. Its strategy for many decades has been to serve its *customers* through its *capabilities*, which are founded in its *competencies*. The combined effect of three well-fitted or complementary Cs in the market is what makes Lincoln a truly formidable competitor.

Lincoln expands its competencies by solving customers' welding problems as they arise. Lincoln learned early on that the keys to competence building are to be open to learning and to invest in that learning. Its management steadily invests in training, in field-based research through its consultant sales engineers (who know enough to say, Let me show you what I am talking about), and in capacity and capability enhancements.

Applying 3C Thinking

What an organization sees and learns is shaped by the questions it asks. When asking questions about the future, customers, competencies, and capabilities, the 3Cs are seen as resources that we already have to compete with. But when asking questions about past performance, the same 3Cs are viewed as results achieved, enhanced through learning garnered from prior action in the market. When Lincoln enters one of its problem-solving situations, their established welding competence is a resource to be used. Their ability to gain the customer's confidence and to learn how to solve a new welding problem can be seen, looking backward in time, as one result of having already built an existing customer relationship. This dual nature of the 3Cs, then, is that they are first garnered from feedback that is recognized and captured through organizational learning and, then, converted by management decisions and effort into a new, expanded, or differentiated basis for competition and strategic change. This is why a company's assessment of its own 3C balance (or 3C alignment) is a severe test for any future strategy or opportunity.

The dual nature of each of the 3Cs, while possibly somewhat confusing at first, is not a manifestation of a new business philosophy. It simply extends a familiar notion from finance to a wider multifunctional and multi-process domain. Every businessperson knows that financial results beget financial resources. Financial results include the cash that flows to the company. The retention of earnings expands the balance sheet, thus providing additional resources to fund the company's operating and strategic decisions. So it is with the 3Cs. Indeed, the dual nature of the 3Cs, and the critical role of managing feedback in the conversion of results to resources, is easier to appreciate if one sees corporate results as more than cash flow, sales, and earnings, or market-share points. Instead, widen the definition of results to include relationships built, competencies expanded by learning, and capabilities acquired and refined by use.

In Lincoln's case, it is a unique competence that its field staff has mastered—how to learn from their customers, bring questions and new solutions home, and then instruct them in turn. (You may be aware of a similar competence enjoyed by Toyota worldwide, both within its plants and with all of its suppliers.) This competence at organizational learning depends on Lincoln's having access to its customers' workshops, factories, and business processes, and behaving as if these were their shared enterprise's real research laboratories. Its customer relations are a resource for its new product development process. Similarly, its ability to use volume to cut its unit costs feeds back into its order acquisition process to result in lower prices. Likewise, Lincoln Electric's low staff turnover—the average employee experience in its manufacturing plants is more than ten years, despite substantial growth—cuts recruiting and training costs, thereby reducing overhead. This cost advantage stems, in large part, from the company's human resources management ability (a competence) to simultaneously reward piecework while encouraging innovation, quality output, and continuous improvements within its manufacturing (fulfillment processes). Lincoln's consistent approach has earned the company its employees' trust, with the happy result that the company retains a highly experienced, cost-cutting workforce whose competence multiplies its capabilities and boosts its customer services while allowing price cuts.

Lincoln's 3Cs align seamlessly. As shown in Figure 3-3, the three boxes that highlight customers, competencies, and capabilities are not only linked over time through each operating cycle but are well aligned strategically over the longer term and are in balance with the company's customer reach.

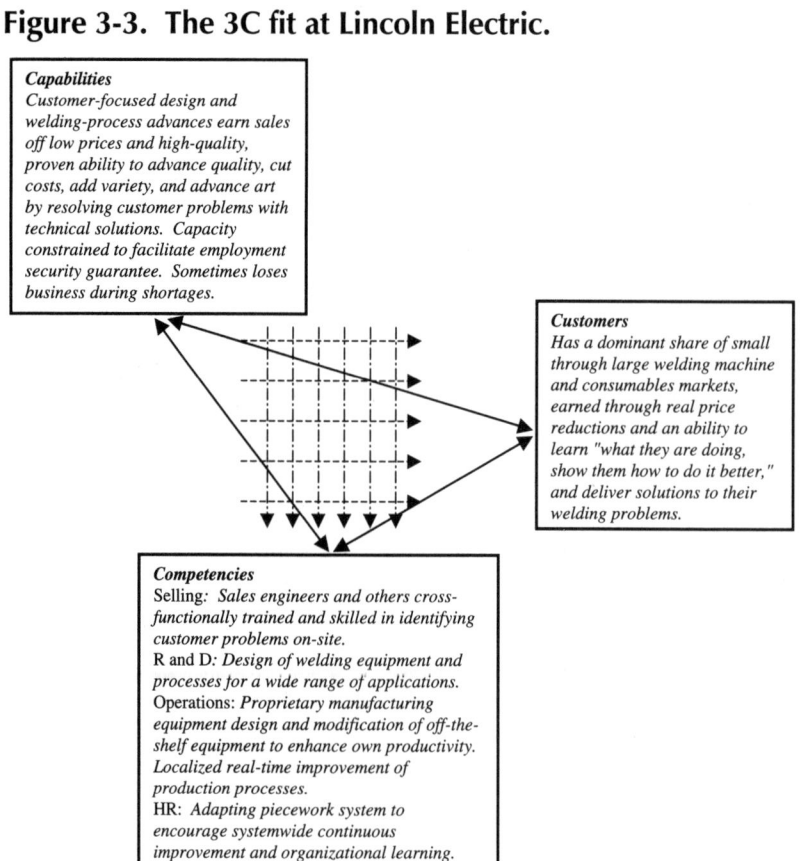

Figure 3-3. The 3C fit at Lincoln Electric.

Capabilities
Customer-focused design and welding-process advances earn sales off low prices and high-quality, proven ability to advance quality, cut costs, add variety, and advance art by resolving customer problems with technical solutions. Capacity constrained to facilitate employment security guarantee. Sometimes loses business during shortages.

Customers
Has a dominant share of small through large welding machine and consumables markets, earned through real price reductions and an ability to learn "what they are doing, show them how to do it better," and deliver solutions to their welding problems.

Competencies
Selling: Sales engineers and others cross-functionally trained and skilled in identifying customer problems on-site.
R and D: Design of welding equipment and processes for a wide range of applications.
Operations: Proprietary manufacturing equipment design and modification of off-the-shelf equipment to enhance own productivity. Localized real-time improvement of production processes.
HR: Adapting piecework system to encourage systemwide continuous improvement and organizational learning.

When viewed as resources, the 3Cs allow you to focus on the critical elements of the fit between your evolving customer base and your company's resource platform, that is, on its existing process capabilities, functional competencies, and customer relationships. The Lincoln Electric example shows how knowledge of each C can help managers discuss their enterprise's market positioning. Hence, the balance between the 3Cs—customer expectations, functional competencies, and process capabilities—defines the feasibility of your objectives and future strategy.

We recommend engaging your management team in the assessment of your 3C balance to refocus their thinking on your customers, competitors, and the possibility of partnering with other companies. In particular, we have found that when management has a tendency to look inward, they are likely to find the internal audit from Chapter 2 quite engaging. That internal node-by-node sharing of knowledge can focus management's attention on its internal affairs and problems so intensely that external contracting and partnering options may be temporarily forgotten in a drive to optimize the internal systems and resolve their problems. So now you can deal with this possibility using 3C thinking to look at the enterprise level and consider the competencies and capabilities of your own organization, along with current and potential contractors and partners as they combine to serve your customers. This 3C check across the value chain reminds you why you are making the effort to know where your company stands—the optimization of the enterprise itself, not the optimization of a particular business process within it.

Opportunities for Contracting and Partnering

Enterprise leaders are now learning to deliberately build organizational competencies to gain the competitive edge, declining to own anything except a few select steps in the value-adding chain while divesting chunks of their supply chain's tangible assets. For example, in the 1990s, the new-product realization process was formalized converting informal know-how at the individual level to an organizational competency. In the manufacturing industries, this process led to a smoother flow of new product introductions and a more predictable innovation process. The development of integrated supply chains, with their accompanying ERP software systems, creates other process capabilities and has redefined the sources of competitive advantage in many markets.

Throughout the global electronics industry, where the rate of product obsolescence is high, the reduced cost and increased speed of fulfilling customer orders depends in part on contract manufacturing specialists like Solectron, Jaybil, and Celestica. Indeed, the staggering growth of contract manufacturing, in this and other industries, occurred because many traditional manufacturers realized that they were too vertically integrated to be flexible, too exposed to the risk of obsolescence, and lacking in specialized organizational competencies that they needed to win. The Internet and associated software, as noted earlier, has provided yet another technology for enterprise leaders to employ to combine their partners' competencies and process capabilities with their own, creating supply chains that are even more abbreviated in both time and cost. Dell Computer became an enterprise leader and a success in the highly competitive PC market by choosing a business model that engaged select component designers and manufacturers but reserved for itself the high value-adding final assembly step, along with highly automated processes for order acquisition and customer service.

The decision to perform one business process internally or to contract it wholly (or in part) to another entity, as Dell has done, is important and complex. Despite the costs and energy required, the internal route offers advantages of direct control and the preservation of potentially valuable options for future action. On the other hand, the advantages of contracting can be conceived in terms of costs, flexibility, enhanced competitive advantage for the enterprise as a whole, and possibly, different valuable real options if the contracted processes can be integrated into a unified enterprise by its leader. Each contract/do decision must be based on a review of process capabilities, functional competencies, and the time required to manage the work flow—whether in-house or contracted—rather than on classical investment criteria and incremental needs for material, labor, capital, and capacity.

Of course contracting out has its costs, both tangible and intangible. First, integrating a contracted business process with those performed internally usually requires an investment in IT systems to link the two in real time. There are also the normal management costs associated with a contracted-out business process: the energy and attention needed to control results, identify improvement opportunities, manage conflict between the organizations involved, and overcome potential problems associated with maintaining the security of proprietary knowledge.

Finally, there is the challenge of trying to influence the development of future capabilities by each contractor to fit the projected needs and dealing with the day-to-day issues, such as maintaining control as goods or services are handed off from one company to another in the value chain. We call this last problem crossing the "white space." If you have ever been a hospital patient being transferred from one unit or department to another, you have probably had to live in your own white space where no one is exactly in charge and no one is explicitly responsible for your welfare. Great companies eliminate troublesome white spaces when they are discovered, thus ensuring that their customers consistently experience timely and accurate responses.

The impact of contracts and the problem of setting up fast, consistent, and reliable business processes, no matter the load, is part of the rivalry between Amazon.com and Barnes and Noble in the book business. Amazon has an extraordinary order acquisition process but mostly relies on other sources for fulfillment. Initially, there was the wholesaler, which operates at a very low margin with high volume. Then, there is shipping by Federal Express, United Parcel Service, and others. All along this chain are opportunities for slipups that can impact Amazon quite seriously. The much heralded release of the fourth Harry Potter book in the summer of 2000 saw Amazon in the news, and in trouble, because 3,800 of several hundred thousand orders were late. Instant ordering appears to imply close to instant delivery with total acuity in the Internet world, which is, of course, one of the reasons why Amazon had expanded its warehouse system—even though that is an investment in the old economy and puts its future growth in question.

By this point, we hope you have a useful sense of both the 3Cs and the advantages and risks of contracting and partnering business processes. Now we turn to the challenging problem of creating a networked enterprise and leading it. The company we will discuss, Calyx & Corolla, was chosen for illustrative purposes only and is not intended to signal preferred solutions to other business situations. Nonetheless, we hope that this discussion will trigger questions that you can use to shape your own organization.

The Calyx & Corolla Example

Calyx & Corolla offers a nice illustration of the power of customer-centered thinking. From the start, the Calyx &

Corolla business model focused on a single networked enterprise in which all key participating entities could be winners, while the company, through its leadership role, could capture a disproportionately high return on the capital invested.

In 1987, Ruth Owades decided to start a new business, Calyx & Corolla, with a clear mission: to provide fresh flowers, at a reasonable cost, direct to designated individuals from customers who ordered by telephone. Within five years, the company was achieving annual sales of more than $20 million, with the help of only a dozen or so full-time employees. The company worked in partnership with thirty growers located in California, Florida, and Hawaii, and utilized the services of Federal Express, which handled all product distribution. From the outset, Ruth Owades embraced a customer-centered business model based on "customer pull." In this model, catalog sales trigger orders and pull flowers directly from the grower before being sent to the intended recipient.

Taking a Business Process View

Calyx & Corolla is an example of a well-designed, lean, customer-centered enterprise. It chose its products and markets carefully, and then designed a process structure to win. Owades created the full Calyx & Corolla enterprise carefully by enrolling leading-edge partners to perform most of the capital-intensive process work. She chose to meet Calyx & Corolla's business objectives with a minimum requirement of new capital. Calyx & Corolla handles four of the five generic business processes as follows:

▲ *New Product Development*—Calyx & Corolla's employees identify new flower-related products, based on a keen market sense. They contract with and train growers or other suppliers (artificial flowers, etc.) to conform to

Calyx & Corolla's quality specifications, and design six catalogs a year that display these new products (along with the familiar ones).

▲ *Order Acquisition*—Calyx & Corolla's employees take orders by telephone and transmit them to select growers.

▲ *Order Fulfillment*—Growers, trained by Calyx & Corolla, put the desired flower arrangements in Calyx & Corolla–specified packaging, specially designed to minimize damage, which are then promptly picked up by Federal Express and delivered overnight.

▲ *Post-Sales Service*—Calyx & Corolla employees instruct the recipients of flowers in flower care, remind customers of special family days, and keep the catalogs coming.

These four business processes are all vital to the long-term success of Calyx & Corolla. We can say that Calyx & Corolla is customer-centered because they see these business processes as the organizational elements to be managed, monitored, and improved. You can note that since all of Calyx & Corolla's sales are via credit card, the company has essentially contracted out the credit and collections process.

Seizing Enterprise Leadership

The first point to notice about this example is that Owades positioned Calyx & Corolla to be an enterprise leader without investing the huge amount of capital that might have been required to become a successful, traditional, full-line enterprise, integrated through ownership, rather than by negotiation and agreement. Instead of owning each business process, Owades was the entrepreneur who marshaled the resources needed to realize her business concept. She selected her process portfolio and business partners carefully to create this new multicompany enterprise. She negotiated with other organizations—that already had critical competencies in place—to do what she could not do by herself. Her ability to get her way in these negotiations derived from her company's ability to generate and manage a new demand stream that could result in a new, profitable business for the partners, without their having to assume much risk should this enterprise fail. Equally important, she continued to invest her executive energy in making each of these business processes perform superbly in its own right and, most significantly, together as one seamless enterprise by managing it intensely by "walking around."

As Calyx & Corolla shows, process centering can extend beyond the single company situation discussed in Chapter 2 and, with appropriate information technology, can be used to ensure enterprise-wide alignment across many partner companies. Calyx & Corolla's own telecommunication capability, augmented by Federal Express's, is a good example of how such an expanded enterprise can function as one entity. (The Internet is now offering even more cost-effective and rapid options.) Success can be measured, partner by partner, by productivity gains, and by the shortened cash cycles the partners enjoy from their seamless connection.

Owades identified, for each of the core business processes, the capabilities she needed to turn her vision into a competitive reality. In doing this, she had to consider critical interactions between business processes, such as the value of the customer service process in generating new orders and ideas for new products. Finally, she needed full knowledge of her partners' internal process strengths and weaknesses, and the potential availability of these process capabilities to other companies that are or could be her competitors. Being able to envision the 3C balance of competitors with respect to her own customers was as important as the 3C balance of Calyx & Corolla.

Identifying the Core Business Processes

Enterprise leadership at Calyx & Corolla was aimed at acquiring a growing base of loyal customers for increasing the amount of business over the years—the repeat customers. The rationale for this definition comes from the economics of the mail order, direct-delivery, retail business. Profit is made on repeat purchases while cash is expensed in the costly search for new buyers. Therefore, although all four business processes are essential to Calyx & Corolla's long-term business success, can one be identified as the true source of its enterprise leadership? In other words, what is the one business process that will most directly *win* the growth of this enterprise while the other business processes *qualify* Calyx & Corolla to compete for that potential growth?

We see the real cutting-edge business process—once Calyx & Corolla was up and running—as being new product development. Performance in this business process enables every partner in the extended Calyx & Corolla enterprise to satisfy their shared customers and incrementally improve what they are already doing well. Without new products, Calyx & Corolla would be limited by the sales potential of their initial set of flower arrangements. By expanding the enterprise's product offering, new products provide an engine for growth by providing something different to send to customers' loved ones. And new complementary products—vases, artificial flowers—generate still more business from loyal customers. Thus, the process of new product development helps ensure that, by being differentiated from its competitors, the Calyx & Corolla enterprise has an opportunity to build its profitable base through repeat customers, even if competitors adopt a comparable business model with similar logistic capabilities. Calyx & Corolla has no choice but to build its internal competency with fast cycle processes for developing and introducing new products.

Order fulfillment, however, is also a determinant of business success for Calyx & Corolla. After all, how many experiences with errors will a customer tolerate before ceasing to do business with Calyx & Corolla? And what kinds of errors can occur? Wrong flowers, damaged or wilted flowers, and late delivery immediately come to mind. The founder of Calyx & Corolla decided at the outset to contract with a set of reliable quality flower growers, who would pick and pack arrangements on a made-to-order basis. Calyx & Corolla also decided to stay out of the delivery end of the business, and so developed an arrangement with Federal Express to pick up all orders at the growers' locations and deliver them directly to specified recipients. These decisions to "contract" were easy to make, given the start-up nature of Calyx & Corolla, the special investments and competencies required either to grow flowers in volume or to execute flawless overnight delivery of parcels, and, of course, the availability of such suppliers. Furthermore, the contracts with the growers and Federal Express were conceived and negotiated as partnership relationships, rather than as at-arm's-length, price-based contracts. Calyx & Corolla also maintained other less strategic contracts with suppliers of basic materials and printing services, providing us with a model that we might be able to emulate and adapt to our own circumstances.

Achieving 3C Balance

To ensure direct customer contact and to tap customers for feedback, Owades chose to handle the order acquisition process internally. Calyx & Corolla hired staff to handle the incoming orders, adding employees as demand grew and providing them all with homegrown training. Building upon Owades' prior experience in another catalog-driven direct marketing business, Calyx & Corolla chose to develop from the start a competency in catalog design, new product ideas, and the handling of post-sales service calls from customers. By choosing to display their offerings of exotic flowers in a beautiful catalog that was designed in-house, Calyx & Corolla made a valuable investment in promoting customer satisfaction: customers placing orders from their home or office could actually see in advance what they would get. This also helped them provide another form of distinctiveness in their service to customers—a previously unheard-of, money-back guarantee.

Calyx & Corolla could offer a money-back guarantee even though they had chosen not to do any of the order fulfillment process themselves. By working with reliable growers and Federal Express—both of whom had large incentives for doing their process activities in a superior manner and were unlikely to expand into Calyx & Corolla's business space as direct competitors—Calyx & Corolla greatly reduced the risk of this service guarantee.

Calyx & Corolla reduced its risk exposures even further by choosing to do the following critical activities themselves:

- Providing critical training to the growers on how to aesthetically arrange the flowers in packing cartons, and how to include a handwritten gift card from the sender to the recipient.
- Providing growers with demand forecasts and with needed materials that they maintained in their warehouse (such as shipping cartons, gift cards, labels, and vases).
- Ensuring that the packing boxes were designed to maintain freshness and avoid damage in transit.
- Investing in information technology to integrate the

order fulfillment process and allow the enterprise to guarantee exact day delivery (to coincide with special occasions) rather than a uniform next day (after the order is placed) delivery.

Hence, despite their heavy reliance on partnership relationships with the growers and Federal Express, plus other contracts for materials and printing, Calyx & Corolla positioned itself to be firmly in charge as the enterprise leader. Ruth Owades and her small management team invented a new business model. They reconfigured the industry supply chain as a system pulled by customer demand and operated to achieve customer satisfaction. They marshaled the resources to win and set new industry standards of product freshness, delivery speed, and convenience by creating a new, vital, and 3C-balanced multicompany enterprise.

Their needs for capital were minimal because they contracted with a carefully selected set of partners with the needed competencies, capabilities, and capacity for order fulfillment. And, they supported these order fulfillment partnerships with strategic but low levels of capital investment, concentrating their management energy on order acquisition, product development and customer service. Finally, because Calyx & Corolla's partners were not likely to become their future competitors, they could freely share information with them and even help them do their own jobs better. Not every partnership is characterized by integrity on both sides and perfectly consistent mutual interests.

The Risks of Contracting and Partnering

Calyx & Corolla is a simple illustration of contract/do decisions, which are a more general version of make/buy decisions that have application to all business processes, not just order fulfillment. You may have faced the traditional make vs. buy decision in manufacturing, possibly determining the tactics of production using a one-dimensional criterion—such as return on investment. In contrast, there are likely to be considerable subtleties and risks embedded in contract/do decisions.

Of course the contract/do decision has been perceived as strategic from the start. Yet, such decisions are still often fragmented into smaller elements and buried within the agendas of one or another function. Examples of inappropriate one-by-one decisions include: contracting for IT systems, customer satisfaction surveys, executive development programs, customer support activities, and the field service of installed equipment. In a truly customer-centered organization, such contract/do decisions need to be made by executives responsible for the entire business process who have the ability to see connections with other business processes, and to make such choices in broadly competitive terms. This is best accomplished, as we suggested in Chapter 2, by emphasizing the sharing of knowledge within the corporate and enterprise management teams who bear the risk.

Making Contract/Do Decisions

Several risk factors shape the strategic contract/do decision, among them are financial implications, human capital, the risk of hollowing out, cost/value trade-offs, and various hard and soft costs associated with contracting and doing the business processes. We will review these one by one:

▲ *Traditional Financial Considerations.* Contracting cuts the property, plant, and equipment (PP&E) required by the company on the buying side of the contract. Investments in information technology support should reduce requirements for working capital on both sides of the contract, as close to real time information eliminates need for buffer inventory and shortens the cash-to-cash cycle. Significantly, too, the heavy reliance on IT to streamline business processes should ultimately cut personnel costs company-by-company within the enterprise.

▲ *Competencies and Human Capital.* The new economy investments in knowledge can be even more competitively significant in the long run than investments in working capital or PP&E. Thus, enterprise leaders need to consider the need for human as well as physical assets, and the value of selective investment in human resources (coupled with IT support). Before deciding to abandon specific process-relevant competencies to achieve short-term cost cutting, you must consider whether to do so would imply forgoing options that could provide the enterprise with the needed flexibility to survive an unknown future.

▲ *Hollowing Out.* One risk that every manager needs to be aware of is called hollowing out. Many long-established companies are reducing their asset base so dramatically as e-commerce grows that they face the possibility of a rapid demise if they have become hollowed out. Hollowing out is the condition of a firm that is so dependent on suppliers and other contractors that it no longer possesses the internal competencies and capabilities to protect and build a competitive advantage and, so, is in danger of losing its freedom to be self-determining. In identifying opportunities to contract and partner, therefore, you should be sensitive to this danger, especially when you face pressure to limit investment or to cut head count.

▲ *A Key Cost and Value Trade-Off: Capacity and Proprietary Knowledge.* The enterprise leader needs to consider how the process ownership decision should be affected by the two factors of cost of capacity and value from proprietary knowledge. Cost of capacity is the total of one-time investments and ongoing direct expenditures that are necessary (inputs) to achieve the needed rate of output over the planning horizons of the company or enterprise. Value from proprietary knowledge is measured in terms of profit streams that are likely to accrue over the planning horizon from a winning and inimitable business process. The greater the significance of unique knowledge in the competitive arena, the more the businesses involved will use relational exchanges—for example, partnerships—rather than simple price-based contracts, and the greater the role of integrity in resolving any disputes that may arise. The more tightly that competitive advantage is tied to certain unique knowledge assets, the more seriously the enterprise leader should consider investing in creating them as foundations for internal business processes rather than in contracting them out.

Figure 3-4 catalogs these trade-offs and lists the likely strategies within each of several knowledge-defined spaces. In general, when the cost of capacity additions rises, you will be less inclined to make the necessary investment and should consider strategies that are more capital-efficient. Normally under such circumstances, you will seek contracting arrangements that result in your company owning a reduced portion of the business process. Note, however, that as the value of proprietary knowledge rises to significant levels, most companies will prefer to own those processes, even if the costs of acquiring incremental capacity are high. Also, there is some minimum threshold of proprietary knowledge, beneath which a simple price-based contract will always be preferable. This is especially so when the cost of building this process capacity rises.

▲ *Hard vs. Soft Costs.* Contract/do decisions will always be affected by a combination of the "hard" investment cost of gaining the needed capacity and the "soft" cost of the executive energy needed to achieve the desired outcome. Depending on the option selected, your

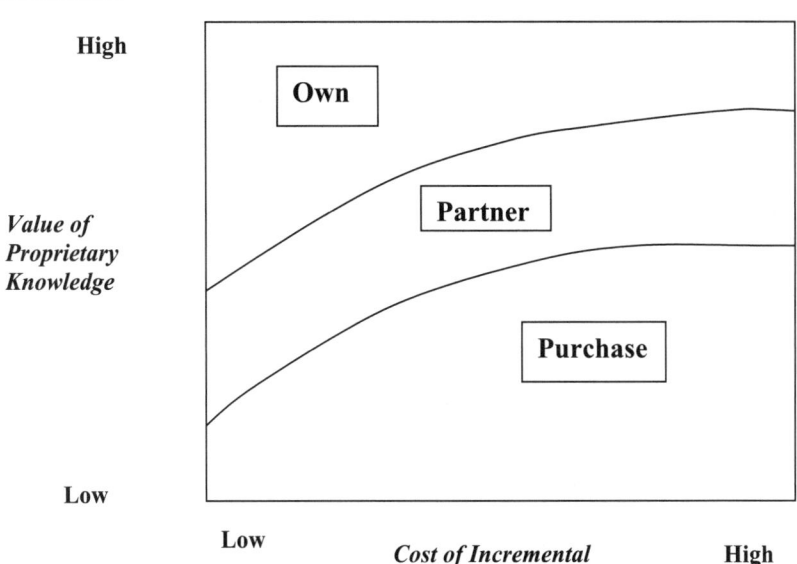

Figure 3-4. Knowledge, capacity, and the contract/do decision.

Y-axis: Value of Proprietary Knowledge (Low to High)
X-axis: Cost of Incremental Capacity (Low to High)
Regions: Own (upper left), Partner (middle), Purchase (lower right)

actual costs will vary. In any event, the elements of hard costs include: capital investment required to build the capacity to manage the demand forecast over the planning horizon; related investments in working capital, information technology, and human capital; and payments to contractors.

Also necessary, but harder to measure, are the soft costs of allocating your scarce executive energy for promoting the development of critical knowledge assets; developing and overseeing a business process, and improving it as needed over time; negotiating and maintaining critical partnership relations; and selecting and monitoring the contracted works. Given the range and variety of the soft cost elements, you will need to pay careful attention to cost measurement as a prerequisite for conducting meaningful trade-off analysis. Further, the aggregate executive energy required for each of your contract/do choices needs to be considered independently. Executive energy may turn out to be the scarcest and so, the most limiting resource.

Positioning Your Organization for Enterprise Leadership

Weighing these factors carefully will help you identify the business processes and partners you need to service your customers. Doing so positions you for enterprise leadership. In practice, we recommend that you and your team start with a broad, subjective 3C assessment, sharing knowledge and summarizing the discussion using relative ratings (high, medium, and low). Once this exercise has begun, it may quickly become clear that the business process being considered for outsourcing is actually composed of several subprocesses, much like Calyx & Corolla found in the flowers-by-phone industry. Each of these is likely to deserve its own contract/do assessment. The objective is to accomplish enough quick and dirty screening so that some decisions are easy to pin down without further analysis. Then, in a second pass, the same instrument panel can be calibrated, with more precise measures, to support final choices among the available options and partners.

Recall that Calyx & Corolla preferred to contract and purchase a large proportion of the services and products needed to fulfill its customers' needs. In contrast, your company may prefer to do more internally if you can make a case for this investment-intensive configuration. Such a case is likely to deal with the limited availability of suitable potential partners and the competitive value of building the new knowledge needed to maintain leadership in particular business processes.

Avoid ideological positions on business process ownership. The proper answer to the question of what and how

Checking Feasibility: Customers, Capabilities, and Competencies   75

much to own will depend on the overall competitive situation. In the short term, this might be rephrased as, How can we create the most advantaged enterprise while keeping our own resource base lean and limiting our risks? From a longer-term perspective, you will need to consider the risk and costs of hollowing out, where you have failed to build some distinctive competencies due to an overreliance on external contracts. In other words, you want to avoid ending up with critical competency gaps that threaten your future competitive success.

Watch out, also, for the opposite situation, where you unwittingly help a potential future competitor to build its own competencies. This may occur when your company transfers knowledge and technology to a partner or supplier in the process of creating a stronger enterprise. Traditionally, IBM and Boeing, for example, have been careful to design careful barriers for knowledge transfer with their project suppliers so that they control the knowledge that moves on a need-to-know basis. Among their concerns was the knowledge needed to manage very large-scale projects as well as technology. Such care reduces the chances that sometime in the future such technology or knowledge could become a competitor's core competency, and be offered at a lower cost, thereby nullifying the advantage you currently enjoy. Along these lines, note that Calyx & Corolla had little cause for concern that their partners—flower growers or Federal Express—would use the knowledge they gained to independently enter the catalog-based fresh flower delivery business as Calyx & Corolla's competitors. The growers lacked capital and management capability while Federal Express had its own incentives to build a logistics service business with integrity.

Strategically sound process decisions will shift from price arrangements to relationship-based partnerships, and then to process integration and ownership as knowledge yields greater advantage. The prospects for relationship-intensive partnerships, which are based on quality management principles and integrated information technology, can be significant. On the other hand, it is also important to assess the likely degree of cultural fit between your organization and those of your partners. Mismatches in this critical dimension can be fatal, even when all the parties agree to proceed with the partnership.

Considering all of these factors, it is clear that the key to success in this critical contract/do decision sequence is getting the right people to share the specialized knowledge they have about every one of the underlying factors. If you build a particular business process internally, to what extent will this promote the success of the enterprise and the chances of your achieving competitive advantage? If the motivation to own the process is quite low in both dimensions, then check for a viable contracting option, especially when there are no major interconnections with other internal processes. If the motivation is quite high, then explore the various hard and soft cost dimensions to check that they can be justified, given the potential advantage of owning that process. If the motivation is mixed from the first two factors, then assess all the options to reach a preliminary conclusion as to whether ownership or partnership contract seems more desirable.

In summary, ask your executive team to look at the pattern of process advantages and constraints across these factors to decide whether and how to participate in this business process of the broader enterprise. Some patterns may be easy to interpret while others may be difficult. For some, there will be no difficulty in accepting the initial, and most subjective, reading, while for others closer scrutiny may be needed. When the full set of business processes has been subjected to this analysis, the first pass in determining your enterprise leadership position will be completed.

Conclusion

The 3C test determines whether your target customers are being served with competitive advantage due to the combined set of functional competencies and process capabilities of your organization and your key contractors and partners. The decision to perform a business process internally or to contract it wholly (or in part) to another entity is, therefore, an important and complex strategic decision. Making such decisions work is the concern of everyone involved. Despite the costs and energy required, relying on your own process capabilities and organizational competencies offers the advantages of direct control and the preservation of real options. The advantages of contracting, on the other hand, can be conceived in terms of costs, flexibility, enhanced competitive advantage for the enterprise as a whole, and possibly, different valuable real options, if the contracted processes can be integrated into a unified enterprise by its leader. Each contract/do decision must be based on a review of process capabilities, functional competencies, and the time required to manage the work flow—whether in-house or contracted—rather than on classical investment criteria such as incremental needs for material, labor, capital, and capacity.

After your sizing-up of the situation is completed and your present contract/do decisions have been reviewed and perhaps revised, your effort at the enterprise level is not over. For several reasons, you cannot ignore those business processes that are being contracted out (in the sense that one might readily ignore a market segment or R and D option beyond the scope of the current business). First, integrating a contracted business process with one being performed internally usually requires an investment in IT systems to link the two in real time. There are also a host of normal management costs associated with a contracted-out business process: the energy and attention needed to control results, identify improvement opportunities, manage conflict between the organizations involved, and overcome potential problems associated with maintaining the security of proprietary knowledge. Finally, there is the constant challenge of trying to influence the development of future capabilities by each contractor to fit the projected needs.

A traditional management objective is to achieve correctly sequenced internal joint action to meet or exceed customer expectations. Now, thinking from the broader enterprise view, the objective can be seen as coordinating your business processes with selected business processes that are controlled by other organizations, and carefully managing all handoffs to meet the customer's final expectations. Our "size up" at the enterprise level is a key step in clarifying your current strategy—that is, knowing where you stand—including your choice of partners, the value you and they add, and the profits you can expect. When you make informed choices along these lines, you will free up resources to apply elsewhere as you move ahead and become a truly knowing corporation.

4
Understanding Strategic Stretch

Caterpillar Inc. (CAT) is the world's largest producer of heavy earth-moving equipment. Its traditional business is designing, making, and selling huge earth-moving equipment for large construction and mining projects. The size of the tires on some of their equipment dwarfs the size of its drivers. Caterpillar sells much of its product through major contracts to large construction and mining corporations and to government entities. In 1999, CAT took a big step toward a new formerly unserved customer—small construction or landscaping contractors.

The new business CAT launched supplies a line of compact equipment that is aimed at replacing manual labor. Car-sized machines with construction tools mounted on the front constitute a new class of mobile equipment for tasks such as loading pallets, cutting concrete, or planting trees. The global market for products of this type was estimated to be $4 billion annually, but product prices at around $35,000 are low by CAT standards, so CAT's volume must overcome a slim profit margin. Caterpillar chose to reach that market in the United States through a network of CAT rental stores that are owned by independent dealers. Caterpillar discovered that the competition in this new business is different from what it faces with its traditional product lines.

Clearly, this business initiative represents a strategic stretch for CAT, calling for new sets of products aimed at a new market. And yet, it builds on process capabilities the company already possesses in the areas of product development, manufacturing, and other parts of the order fulfillment process. But is it a stretch configured to win? Or is it destined to be one of those "good ideas" that failed due to capability gaps and inadequate organizational competencies in marketing and distribution? Does Caterpillar's management understand the risks inherent to this new stretch for growth? Do they have plans in place to manage the risks they will face and to learn from the experience?

A knowing corporation will ask and answer such questions before its management commits to any significant stretch initiative. Stretching beyond an established business to new markets is a major step for any company, particularly for its operating managers and employees. It is demanding work for everyone involved, but it is also an opportunity for the organization and its leaders, at every rank, to test their mettle and learn. Tested executives and executive teams are more confident and more capable than those who are untested and, therefore, unproven.

Managing every aspect of a business during a stretch initiative requires all strategy architects and managers to have full knowledge of their business and its capabilities, its competencies and inadequacies, and how they will work together to succeed in the target market. The problem for any organization is to ensure that its operating managers know enough to understand the stretch strategy, to identify and judge its drivers and its limits, and, then, to manage the risks involved. To succeed, the organization must gather together what is known and use this knowledge well. The more widely this knowledge is shared, the wider must be the participation in the stretch effort. Coordination and realignment become easier this way and the prospects of success greater.

We will spend the remainder of this chapter developing your sense of stretch and how to assess its feasibility. Then, in Chapter 5, we will build on your understanding of stretch and deal with risk more specifically, along with the challenge of developing or acquiring the necessary organizational competencies. Use of the methods presented in this chapter and Chapter 5 will facilitate your assessments of your own company's growth strategies and help you play your part in them.

Knowing When to Stretch

When a business is working well, and has satisfied customers and its costs under control, it is time to seek revenue growth and new challenges for management. This means that success is an opportunity to do things right and, therefore, it is time to do more. Doing more with what you have is the intent of stretching. You stretch when your current business is under control and has become efficient enough to have resources available for something new. You stretch the same capabilities that you have already deployed but now apply them in new markets. Therefore, you stretch when you have the capabilities and capacity to venture out beyond your current position without putting the established business and your performance standards or accomplishments at risk. You stretch by using what you have more intently, that is, without substantial investment, and because no capital budget is involved, a manager can often act independently.

Growing your business is supposed to be fun and profitable. However, even in the case of well-funded Internet start-ups, and more commonly in traditional brick-and-mortar companies, aggressive growth through market diversification requires investments in delivery capacity that add risk to the venture. In their enthusiasm for unbounded opportunity, top executives frequently commit to huge strategic stretches. Unfortunately, the result is often breakdown because the stretch proves to be unachievable.

Stretch is only feasible when the needed process capabilities either already exist or are easy to acquire. But it is impossible when critical know-how is unavailable. This chapter will help you know, at the design stage, where you can stretch without breaking, by building on existing capabilities. It will show you how you can appreciate in advance how your enterprise's resource base stands relative to that of your prospective competitions, and how closely you can meet the demands of customers in your prospective target market.

Learning How to Stretch

Once you understand your organization and what it is doing, you will probably see it using two different types of stretch strategy. The least ambitious stretch is to use your capabilities and capacity to help another organization reach its customers more efficiently and with greater advantage. This puts your company on the receiving end of another company's decision to contract rather than to develop this capability itself. You become the partner in the contract/do decision, and your capabilities become part of their solution. In this circumstance, you take on limited management responsibility and allow the other organization to do the coordination and entrepreneurial work. Therefore, you probably do not need an augmented budget or new staff.

When you contract to execute some business process or part of a business process for another company, the degree of stretch involved is relatively small but rarely trivial.

Such ventures can also be opportunities to learn contract administration from the other side. You may also have to expand your capabilities in ways you never anticipated. For example, as described in Chapter 3, when Federal Express became a partner of Calyx & Corolla, its management teams had to learn to deal with a more fragile and perishable parcel—boxed fresh flowers—than they were generally accustomed to handling.

The second and more ambitious type of stretch is also more strategic. It involves reaching out to acquire new downstream or end-user customers on your own account. Here you have to marshal resources that are now underutilized in your established markets and put them to work in another. In this second case, your management team will carry a larger load. Here are some of its possible implications. You will need the competency to establish for yourselves what the new customer requirements are—there will be no other company to do it for you. You may also find that you need specialized new competencies to embody the requirements of your newly targeted customers into your existing products and services. This may overload R and D or manufacturing and the fulfillment process. Failure may overload your service organization. You may even find that you misjudged the degree of stretch involved as you learn more about its customers and the competition. Therefore, you may need to develop new capabilities and competencies for acquiring and fulfilling orders, especially if you have to set up or deal with new distribution channels. As the degree of your planned stretch expands, it is important that you ensure that the required capabilities and capacities either exist or can be readily developed, and that the appropriate information and control systems are in place. You may even find that you need new competencies. You will very likely need to give special attention to building the administrative capabilities needed to carry a more complex set of activities to fruition.

Assessing the Stretch

The evaluation approach we recommend builds on the 3C analysis of Chapter 3. All the concepts, except stretch, should be familiar: customer-centering, process capabilities, and organizational competencies. The basic idea is to carefully define your target customers' performance expectations and, then, assess the feasibility of the stretch you are going to attempt in light of the capability and competency gaps that put you at risk of failure. The issue is to identify any telling gaps in your customer relationships, process capabilities, and organizational competencies vis-à-vis that market. Hence, the use of the 3Cs. And, we recommend doing so before you considering any stretch plan's required capital and its return. It is an approach that stresses reality over fantasy. It is a practical way to "Look before you leap!" and not waste time "cooking the books."

The Concept of 3C Stretch

The essential stretch evaluation question is, Given existing process capabilities and functional competencies, can this company capture this potential target market? Figure 4-1 conceptually depicts the issues in an analysis of this type, using the 3Cs to evaluate a stretch strategy. After describing the generic issues, we will list some examples.

Since it has a well-established customer base (labeled #1), a company with a particular set of capabilities and competencies is trying to assess whether it could easily enter another market (labeled #2), believing that *no new* capabilities or competencies would be needed. The company's emerging business model shows that the competen-

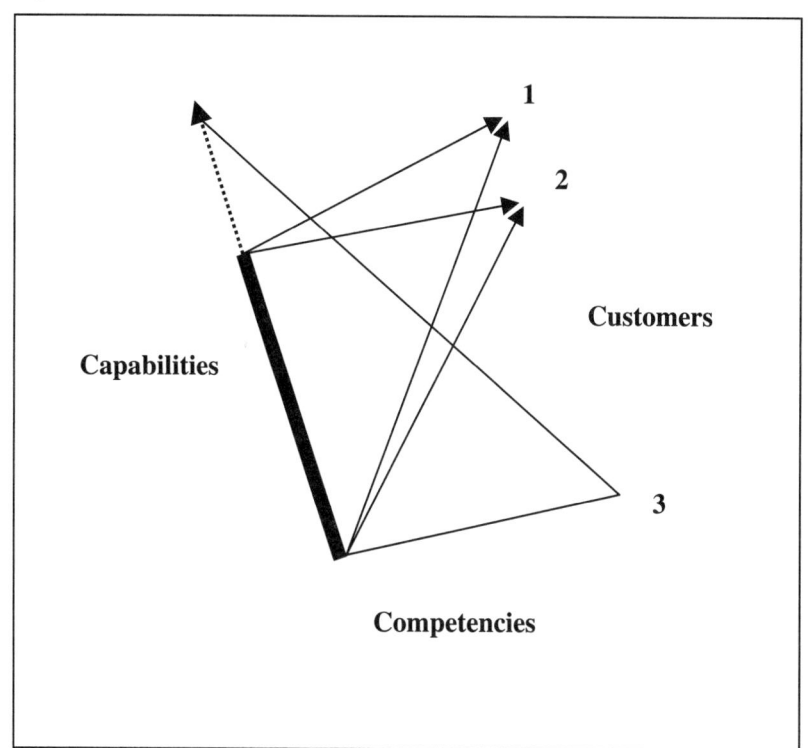

Figure 4-1. 3C stretch assessment.

cies and capabilities now deployed for market #1 could be stretched slightly to do the additional work. Then, the company turned to a different situation represented by market #3. Here it saw the need for significant new capabilities. The company judged #3 as being a substantial stretch. But not because of competency gaps, it simply required new capabilities, as shown in Figure 4-1 by the upward extension of the thick competency/capability resource base to support the move to #3.

An Example of 3C Stretch Analysis

A small Midwestern company faced a situation similar to the one represented here not too long ago. They were leaders in the design and manufacture of prototype and special purpose stainless steel pressure cooking kettles for the food, pharmaceuticals, and cosmetics industries. Their significant sales were consultative—they sold expertise in design along with their ability to manufacture custom kettles. Their order fulfillment worked off a multiweek backlog and employed a highly skilled workforce of artisans who were mostly homegrown. Most orders were for only one or two units. They also sold basic stainless steel tables and serving units to the restaurant industry. This second product line was a more competitive but fruitful business because of the early training received by their uniquely skilled workers, some of whom had twenty-five years of experience.

The company had excellent new product development capabilities, with real competencies in designing high-pressure vessels that worked for their clients' purposes. They had a proven fulfillment capability in this business with good cost control, and usually made reasonably timely deliveries. Quality was high—their product, if maintained as instructed, enjoyed a twenty- to forty-year lifespan. They had limited marketing competencies but took orders graciously from a long list of repeat customers.

Having enjoyed continued success over their first two years in charge, a new management team decided to stretch. They were excited about the commercial and retail potential of a fast-cooking technology that a company engineer had discovered. With the goal of tapping the potential of these two different markets, management was pleased to get orders from a national chicken chain for several ovens to fast-cook turkeys. With their confidence boosted by this initial order, management decided to seek orders for several thousand ovens from their new client and to sell a somewhat simplified version of the oven to the home market.

Figure 4-1 is only symbolic of the changes needed. The

question they should have asked is, "Are we in a #2 or a #3 situation?" It might have helped members of this management team if they had focused their attention on the real problem—identifying the new capabilities needed to succeed in their two new target markets. We will explain why they are #3 target markets, and describe why their prospects of success were very limited indeed. Let us be clear that when the risks of stretch ventures are compounded by stretching unaware, management is often surprised by the results.

You will likely agree that the effort required to stretch from their #1 situation, which was the traditional industrial pressure-cooker prototype business, to what we see as a #2 situation, which is creating the prototype of a new oven for fast-food chain-cooking equipment, was a limited stretch. In this #2 situation, the same competencies used in their long-established business applied, and their workforce, equipment, and new product development and fulfillment processes could easily handle the job.

But setting out to supplying one fast-food chain with several thousand ovens, while simultaneously entering the home market with hopes of selling thousands of counter-space-intense, fast-cooking ovens against the latest microwave and conventional ovens of companies like GE and Amana, is a substantially larger capability stretch. It clearly needs different capabilities across a broader spectrum of business processes and probably new competencies as well to take on these two #3 situations.

Here is how a full but fast 3C assessment might proceed. We will deal with the prospective big order from the chicken chain they were building prototyping for. First, consider the capabilities the new customer—the fast chicken chain—would like to see in a supplier. How? Imagine that you are the project head for the chicken chain's own stretch into the fast fresh-cooked turkey business. You want your product to look and taste right. Hence, you need a tested cooking method and proven oven design. You will need to introduce the new product nationally. You have to equip your restaurants, and there is a lead-time because space needs to be made behind the counter. Before launching the new product, you have to train workers—mostly part-time high school kids—to use the ovens. You have to coordinate the launch with your national advertising campaign, and many other activities.

Now consider what the chain might want from you. How it would measure your performance? Our guess is that the chicken chain wants a few thousand ovens delivered at a modest price almost simultaneously across North America. It will pay on delivery. All the ovens have to work perfectly in the demanding unskilled labor world of the franchised fast-food restaurant. It will want a comprehensive service backup.

Now what capabilities does this imply? What do you need to do to reasonably satisfy this demanding customer? First, you have to be able to manufacture more than a thousand robust and reliable ovens within a narrow window of time, and to do so at low cost. Second, you have to help manage a distributed delivery across North America and meet a sharply defined deadline at each drop point. You may have to help train the people who will teach the chain's employees to use the ovens. And, you will need a rapid-response service delivery capability before you sell an oven to reassure your clients that they can depend on you. After all, they are going to invest many times the price of the oven in their new business venture.

The problem is that our company does not have any of these capabilities. Moreover, it did not have the management capacity or financial resources to proceed. Indeed, the whole idea of the "big order" is a self-enticing fantasy, well removed from reality. Why the effort to stretch? They were focused on the goal and the returns when everything worked out right, rather than on the capabilities needed to win the order in the first place—as seen by their target customer. Without a framework like the 3Cs, they were simply unable to see reality.

Key Questions to Ask

Several practical questions arise that point to ways to extend 3C analysis: If the new market #3 is only emerging now, how long will it take for us to achieve a competitively advantaged position? Are our resources and customer relationships rich and secure enough to allow the simultaneous pursuit of advantage in both our present market and this emerging market? If not, how can we enhance our existing process capabilities and eliminate any capability gaps with respect to both our current markets and new target markets? How taxing will the complexity of dealing with the new market be for our administrative systems and our current management capacity? Do we have the administrative competencies and the will to succeed that we need to win?

Clearly, these questions are not always easy to answer. But that is exactly the point of creating a knowing corporation: to use troubling questions as a lightning rod for creating, sharing, and testing needed knowledge. As leaders in your company, you can use such questions to foster debate about how your entry, or stretch strategy, will build advantage and help make the reality connection.

Likewise, operating managers at every level and in every function can be alert to the information needed to control the effort and ensure that the entry strategy continues to focus on their intended customer. Taken as a set, these questions also ensure that your organization applies the strengths it has and acknowledges its weaknesses before taking its big step forward. The full battery of questions might even extend to asking about the impacts of environmental pressures of every type, for example, the political, economic, social, and technological trends that could affect the success of the stretch strategy.

Note that the stretch evaluation process is focused on the 3Cs as resources for future competition. They give you a quick and early sense of whether your company's aspirations and the new market opportunity being addressed can be balanced with the available resources. The distinctive contribution of the 3C frame in stretch mode is that it allows you to explicitly address the adequacy of the firm's hard and soft resources as strategic decisions are considered, but before the company is committed. Thus far, we have limited the discussion to the hard capabilities of the company, but resources of each type are needed in any strategic change. Executives have told us repeatedly that an enterprise's soft customer relationships and administrative competencies are the most difficult to assess correctly before the action begins. The following account of Lincoln Electric Company's global expansion experience will demonstrate this difficulty.

Stretching to the Breaking Point

Some years ago while speaking to a class at the Harvard Business School, William Irrgang, Lincoln's CEO at the time, was asked what Lincoln would do if welding was displaced by a new unrelated technology. He replied that the company had a doomsday plan to expand its electric motor business, and predicted it would only be a matter of months before Lincoln would dominate its chosen market segments. Using the 3C frame, Lincoln's confidence about its future was rooted in its design and manufacturing competencies and its long-term proven capabilities to make electric motors in-house, since electric motors are an essential component of the arc welder and the company already supplied its own needs. Besides, Lincoln had been founded to make electric motors. Moreover, Lincoln knew who the profitable customers were in this line of business, and believed that the electric motor market would be long-lived. In the electric motor business, Lincoln Electric's 3Cs were balanced prospectively, but this was because the stretch required to implement this plan was limited.

Despite its illustrious history and contingency plans during the 1980s, Lincoln reported losses for the first time in the early 1990s. In fact, management had to borrow to pay its dividend and its bonus to U.S. employees in 1992. Despite continuing success in its U.S. markets, and in its long-established but small Canadian, Australian, and French operations, Lincoln was in trouble after a five-year $325 million global expansion program involving several acquisitions, as well as three new green field plants.

This $325 million multiplant, multicountry, multiacquisition expansion was a huge stretch in more than a financial sense, because the company had only two substantial plants and had done nothing of this ilk before—it had no recent stretch experience. The point is not that Lincoln lacked skills in plant start-ups: In the 1970s, it had launched its second plant in the United States and ramped-up its capacity. However, this had been done quite deliberately, in small incremental steps, and it was overseen by a generation of experienced managers. In contrast, its 1980s expansion program was initiated quickly, in large self-confident steps, based on the company's long-recognized technical and functional abilities and the power of its unique employment system. (The haste was partly in response to a Swedish competitor's acquisitions in the U.S. market.) But when the costs of reunification slowed the German economy and Europe fell into recession, Lincoln's losses began to mount.

In 3C terminology, Lincoln's management had believed it could simply transfer its competencies and process capabilities to European and South American markets and transform or establish its new businesses within a short time. The company's lack of established customer relationships was seen as of little concern. And, with an eye to the value of learning in action, we can note that Lincoln did little to identify its risks by using experiments or tests, or even by following its own long-established tradition of deliberate growth. Not having stretched for a long time, its management simply failed to recognize that stretching can be painful.

By 1992, Lincoln's operations in the United States had been given the task of working the company back to profitability, and most of its global expansion ventures had been shut. In a 1999 postscript, Donald Hastings, the company's chair and CEO through the turnaround years, explained that the company had moved too fast and without deep international experience, and without any real experience in managing at a distance. Hastings wrote that the company simply lacked management depth, ironically because of hiring freezes in the 1960s and 1970s that left the company short of the experienced executives who might have otherwise come to the plate in the 1990s. In our terms, Lincoln was hollowed out. And, unfortunately, its top managers did not realize just how precarious its position was, until the company was stretched to near its breaking point under the pressure of global expansion.

Ultimately, Hastings assigned himself responsibility for operating control in Europe and delegated control of the company's U.S. business to its president, Fred Mackenback. A little luck also helped. As Lincoln struggled to make up for its losses in Europe with new sales in the United States, the U.S. market turned up, and the company's sales rose from a low of about $1.8 million per day up to $3.1 million per day, in only twelve months.

Learning from the Lincoln Example

The lesson for any thoughtful manager is that Lincoln moved unprepared because it had no clear sense of who its customers would be, what they would expect and why, or how to reach them, simply because they had no experience stretching to new markets. They moved without a 3C stretch evaluation, and paid the price.

Rather than being customer-centered, as they had been through their illustrious past, Lincoln had ventured globally almost entirely focused on its own capabilities, and with too little concern for its prospective customers and too limited competency in global marketing and operations. The know-how needed was local to the global market rather than being United States–based.

When appointed CEO, Hastings soon realized that management had put the whole company at risk. The stretch program had substantially burdened the company's administrative systems, a situation exacerbated by the company's simple lack of experienced managers and the administrative competencies needed to manage the strategic task previously committed to with the board's approval of its $325 million capital budget.

Anticipate Competency Gaps

The company fortunately learned from its stretch experience, albeit slowly, since it was under pressure to normalize earnings and cash flow. Its senior managers gained a new appreciation of the contribution that its employees' work-hour flexibility made to its fulfillment process's success in the United States. It learned to sell in Europe. Finally, Lincoln recognized it had limited management depth to compete successfully in the new global economy. The situation was remedied by adding outside directors and recruiting outsiders for senior management positions for the first time in the company's history. Unfortunately, by then, Lincoln Electric had already paid a savage price for lessons learned.

We view Lincoln's transitory failure, not as evidence of a lack of financial capacity or gaps in its functional or technological competencies but rather as evidence of a lack of competency in the global arena. With no market tests or recent stretch initiatives to test and inform its managers, Lincoln found itself with insufficient global administrative competency and management capacity, and so was unable to transfer either its technological competencies or its world-beating process capabilities into its stretch markets. Viewed through a 3C lens, Lincoln had not seen its new ventures as potentially semiautonomous enterprises, and, so, had defined its management needs too narrowly. Accustomed to success in its home markets, Lincoln failed to appreciate the importance of integration across all of its business processes during the expansion attempt.

Move with Deliberate Speed

Lincoln's first step was too big. It was overconfident that its established competencies, processes, and systems in the United States could be transferred and replicated globally. Lincoln failed to see the important role of tacit knowledge and acculturation in creating the seamless integration that characterizes its U.S. operations and is the foundation of its success. Instead, Lincoln apparently tried to establish its new businesses by relying almost exclusively on the capabilities of its order fulfillment process. That this was insufficient for success, as well as being a difficult task in its own right, only became clear when the losses rolled in. And with few customers in these new geographic regions, these ventures had no time for the gradual development of needed capabilities and competencies.

When Lincoln had opened its second U.S. plant in the 1970s, it had proceeded more deliberately with these two sets of factors firmly in mind and, therefore, that expansion worked. But the unsuccessful stretch experiences in the 1980s, and the losses generated by them, may have positioned Lincoln for the knowledge economy better than anyone could have imagined at the time. After all, their failure became a superior, albeit costly, learning opportunity.

Lincoln's experience is testimony that even great companies have problems. Only dead companies have none. This learning experience in the early 1990s may have been Lincoln's perfect preparation for the knowledge economy because the pain of coping with its stretch strategy had opened management's mind to learning. Donald Hastings's leadership style, plus his willingness to listen, led him to ask the questions that generated fresh insights as to the reasons for its successes and problems, and so led to a new understanding of what makes Lincoln distinctive.

Reflect on Your Situation

Do you sense your business unit needs to confront reality more directly? Or do you want to explore small stretch steps of your own with your management team? Either way, you now have an approach for testing your strategic view of new markets. You can seek to create a new balance with these customers by achieving successfully executed and carefully aligned stretches in your enterprise's process capabilities, and owning the necessary organizational competencies. Keep the Lincoln Electric example in mind, as we discuss the steps of the stretch evaluation process that are listed in Figure 4-2. Follow them, and you will be able to stretch without breaking.

Figure 4-2. The stretch evaluation process.

1. Identify the target market.
2. Put yourself in a critical customer's role and decide "what the customer wants."
3. Translate that into the capabilities the customer wants you to demonstrate to get him or her to give you the order.
4. Assess your own capabilities and their capacities. Do you have what the customer wants to see, or are there gaps?
5. If there are no gaps, assess the impact of the stretch needed to win on your existing business and decide how to control the old and the new and where your priorities lie.
6. If there are gaps, ask why. Is it a capacity problem that money can solve or is it a competency issue of gaps or inadequacies? Is it critical? If we move without it, can we learn by starting small? If we go without it, can we win?
7. If the answer is go, stop and think, How do we stand against the existing competitors and their 3C balance? Note that means taking share from their customers; delivering cheaper, better, and faster, and learning more than they know quickly. Can you do it, and how? Is it feasible?

Avoiding Customer Traps

Despite our emphasis on strategic stretch, we must acknowledge that many companies suffer from myopic conditioning, which makes stretch hard to conceive. Having responded with vigor to customer demands to serve them intensely, these companies have lost the vision and ability to adapt and to be self-determining. They exhibit chronic risk aversion as they become captives of their largest customers. This makes them vulnerable to discontinuities in market demand, the acquisition of a large customer by another company, or changes in a customer's top management or strategy. It is easy for these trapped companies to make a strategic error and miss an emerging new market or changes in its old markets.

A well-known example of a company that missed this step in its planning for many years is Xerox. In the 1980s, Xerox became so confident of its success with high-quality, high-priced copying that it deliberately stayed out of the emerging simple, low-service, low-cost copying segment. Fuji Xerox, its affiliate, which was largely restricted in those days to operating in Japan only, saw the same segment as both a threat and an opportunity, and entered it after considerable debate with Xerox's management. Xerox suffered almost a decade of turmoil, in part, because its thinking was "trapped" by its past success—its traditional customers. The company either could not or would not learn from its affiliate and refused to recognize the unserved market as relevant to its future.

Similarly, USX failed to appreciate the emergence of the small, distributed mini-mills as a serious threat for many years since it was trapped by its large high-volume accounts. USX management argued, like so many displaced companies before it, that the quality of its own products was superior, the new technology had limits, it could always improve its own performance when it needed to, and its customers were loyal. Unfortunately for USX, in segment after segment, small scrap-fed electric mini-mill companies like Nucor have proven that they can compete. They have shown they can break out of the initial markets that were ceded to them by USX and its integrated sister companies and break old loyalty barriers with better prices. Their record is continuously improving cost positions. Moreover, they have cut prices, boosted quality, and opened up new segments for themselves by quickly ramping up new technology at economic scale faster than that of the integrated mills.

We have found that the remedy in cases such as Xerox and USX is to challenge management to explicitly identify the potential of the company's unserved markets and to assess whether they are ripe for a stretch entry. Essentially, when taking an exploratory step to verify that the conditions leading to your decision "not to serve" are still valid, the challenge is to find evidence that will ground your current knowledge about your unserved markets and help you appreciate your ability to serve it competitively.

It is a situation faced by perennially successful companies such as Pitney Bowes, which has had a U.S. Postal Service monopoly to manage the franked mail systems for businesses in the United States. With the advent of fax technology and the Internet, it faces the threat of obsolescence. Thus, while it does all in its power to maintain the value of its traditional franchise, Pitney Bowes has ventured into home office and small office markets, stretching to find a path to new future.

Realizing that Opportunity Goes to the Prepared Mind

We cannot organize a business and sustain its success without knowledge. From time to time, we may stumble across a new opportunity, but it is also true that opportunity goes to the prepared mind. Unless we prepare, we will very likely miss opportunity, and fail to capture its principal elements or encode what we do that works. Without preparation, we are likely to lose the advantage gained by discovery as we stretch into the future.

Stretching successfully means moving with the confidence and commitment that knowledge brings. Prepared stretch means knowing where our capabilities stand against the competition, and where we have sufficient edge that we can enter our new market as an innovator. Toward this end, we rely once again on the most potent weapon of the knowing corporation: a good set of questions to guide our inquiry. Who serves the market best? Can we do better still? How? Are our capabilities fully deployed and committed? Are they performing as well as they need to? Is there is any slack or underutilized resource available for experimentation and market testing using our current capabilities? Tests help us define the stretch we will need to enter a new market successfully. They point to ways to develop the competencies and capabilities that we need to win when we finally stretch to accomplish any ambitious market entry.

The Capability/Competency Staircase

Figure 4-3 shows another metaphor for stretching. What will be our staircase to new opportunities? Capabilities are the risers that lift us closer to the markets we seek as we go into action. New or enhanced competencies are the treads on which we stand as we stretch. Together they increase our competitiveness and so are principal elements of the staircase we need to build in preparation for our entry into new markets. By moving deliberately toward our new opportunities—one step at a time—we can limit the stretch we have to make at any point in time so that it never exceeds our breaking point and is, therefore, feasible.

Clearly, our need for capabilities and competencies is shaped by our business strategy, even as capabilities and competencies shape our strategy at the operating level. Remember, too, that capabilities and competencies must be acquired and developed over time to reach the critical mass necessary for a successful entry into a new market.

The staircase represents a dynamic platform for stretching. By thinking about entry as climbing a staircase, you will see stretch defined by both where you are and what you want to reach. Hence, the floating staircase illustrated in Figure 4-3 has some missing elements because it has no beginning, no supports, and an undefined target. It is an omission that confirms the identity of the most impor-

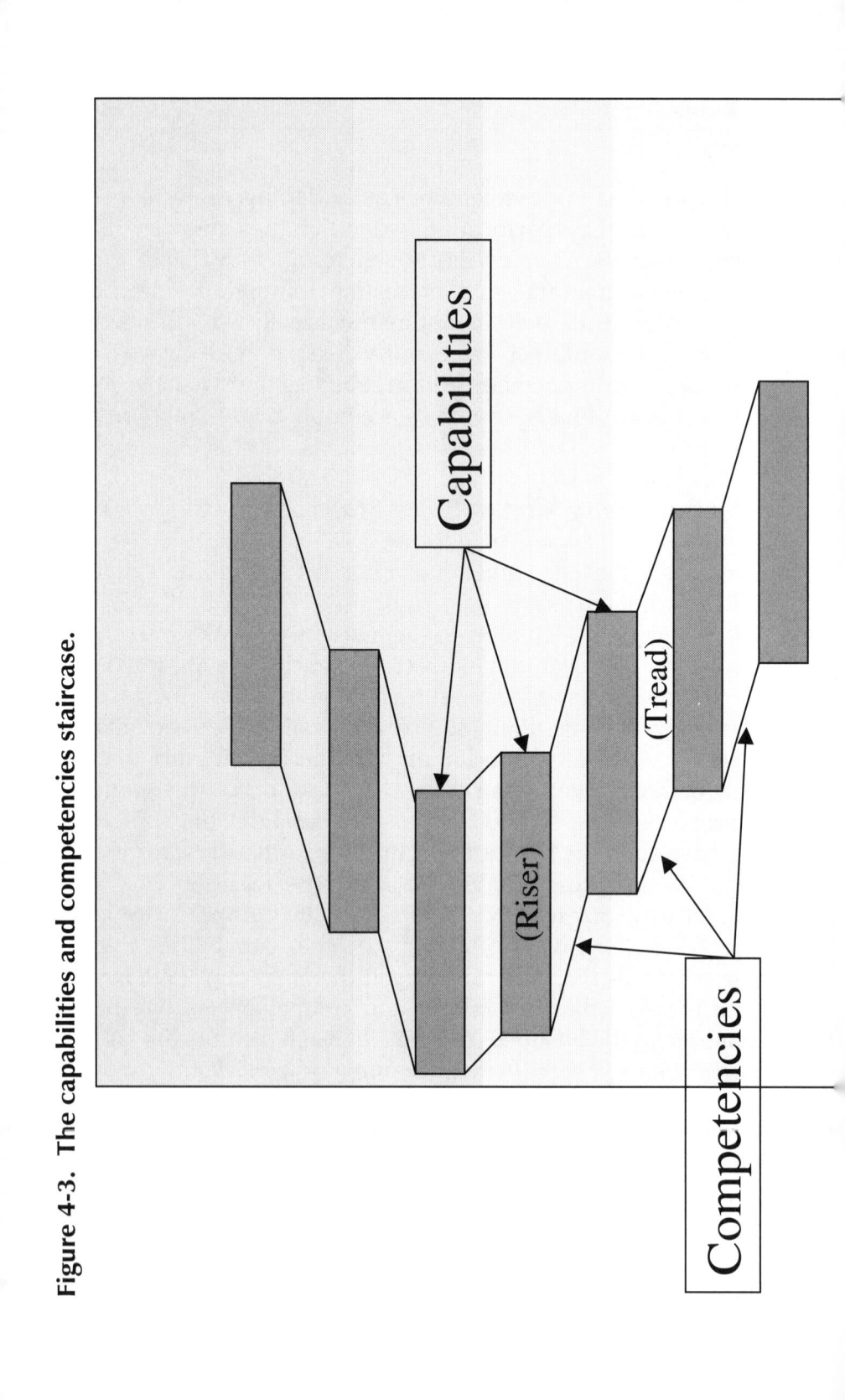

Figure 4-3. The capabilities and competencies staircase.

tant questions that we have to answer. What is our target market? What is the performance they want us to deliver? Remember you have to decide when to move into a market, how far to reach, and how far to stretch. Timing, stretch, and preparation define the risks of your venture. Existing capabilities either empower the effort or limit it.

Application to Internet Companies: eBay

These principles regarding stretching and its risks are of concern to all companies, not just those in traditional, old economy businesses. Even profitable e-commerce companies are under pressure to identify new opportunities to satisfy their shareholders and the capital market's insatiable demands for growth. Consider the situation faced by eBay, the consumer-to-consumer (C2C) auction facilitator. Just like Caterpillar, Lincoln Electric, and Xerox, eBay has had to seek new growth opportunities, even in its early years.

By 1999, eBay's fourth year of business, it was already time to determine when and how it could move beyond the market segments that yielded its first success and stretch itself into new markets. Late in 1999, despite its ongoing pattern of rapidly increasing revenue and profit growth, eBay realized that its growth rate would ultimately decline because the rate of growth of its audience reach was flattening. To complicate matters, eBay had only gone public in 1998 but was blessed with both substantial profitability and large cash reserves, reflecting the success of its business model. The reserves came from earnings and a series of sales of new shares at ever-higher prices, even though the company had little need for capital to expand its C2C business. It required relatively little fixed investment.

One set of possibilities was to venture into the business-to-consumer (B2C) or business-to-business (B2B) auction segments. But the risks eBay would face in such ventures would be compounded by the fact that the company's management depth, while growing, was limited to their own new C2C business. Despite its profitability, eBay was still a very young company with limited customer experience and marketing competencies, a specialized and restricted technology reach, and almost no operations competency. However, eBay enjoyed strong customer loyalty: 20 percent of its total audience were collectors whose repeat transactions constituted about 80 percent of eBay's site volume.

But where were eBay's capabilities and competencies? Because eBay, sensibly, never held title to the goods sold through its Web site, it left order fulfillment completely to its selling customers. Furthermore, they extended no credit other than the receivable fees they charge consumers who sell items through their Web site. They had not yet attempted to develop and introduce new services. All they did was to offer the host site for the auction where their IT system notifies the buyer and seller of the winning bid. Hence, eBay had strong brand equity but was little more than a fully automated Web-based order acquisitions process, supported by a state-of-the-art IT competency. And they were just beginning to find the search for new customers difficult.

The 3C-stretch model suggests that with eBay's narrowly focused competencies, confined customer experience, and limited customer-serving capabilities, any business extension beyond the C2C segment would impose many risks on the company. These limits suggest that extraordinary success in a very specialized business has its price, and that youth, too, has a cost.

Any new business opportunities would bring the need for considerable 3C stretch and associated risk. The reason is that eBay's substantial cash reserve carried risks of its own since their stability and growth could be interpreted by investors as evidence that management either was unable to identify suitable new growth opportunities or that the company lacked the management capabilities or courage to venture forth. In other words, underutilized capital signals that opportunities may be either waning or wasting, auguring a stock price decline.

Meg Whitman, eBay's CEO, was, therefore, in a situation rather like the film or television studio boss who must contend with the aftermath of a huge hit. When there is available cash in the film and television industries, it becomes increasingly difficult to say no to imitative projects and sequels that are almost inevitably going to have lesser returns since their costs will rise and the viewers will sooner or later tire of the genre. The situation at eBay was also complicated by the strong sense of community that its users shared and the importance of trust in their dealings with each other. Trust, however, is a fragile commodity that can be damaged by mishaps on the road to innovation. For all these reasons, restraint in stretching to new opportunities seemed advisable for eBay because the questions of what to do next and how to decide were complicated by their own prior success.

At press time of this book, we still did not know how eBay would ultimately proceed, but have noted that it has only made a few, very likely exploratory acquisitions of other C2C auction businesses. Its objectives seem to be to increase its share in the market segment of high-priced items, where net income earned by the company is expected to be substantially higher than on its average fifty-dollar sale. For example, in September 2000, eBay tried to auction another small e-commerce corporation. It has also entered other small, specialized auction markets, such as the market for antique and classic cars.

Applying the 3C test to eBay shows that it is proceeding carefully and with restraint. It has not fallen into the trap of allowing Amazon.com's entry into the person-to-person auction business to define its own strategy. And it is not stretching to its breaking point. Instead, it is leveraging its current business model by replication, that is, by building strong new customer relationships of the types that it understands. Its existing technological capabilities will probably be sufficient to allow such entries or stretch initiatives with limited investment. And it will probably be able to use its established competencies for some time without further development.

What their stretch ventures cannot do so far, however, is to quickly prepare eBay for a larger-scope venture since they cannot be used to build the new competencies and management capabilities needed. It appears, therefore, that eBay still has to define a new and greater opportunity to ensure the continuity of its greater than 40 percent growth rate and its high price-earnings ratio. How eBay shapes its longer-term strategy and creates its own capability/competency stair to reach that future is an intriguing question at this point. And much the same could be said of most other new economy start-up companies—they need to master the art of the strategic stretch.

The Value of the Stretch Evaluation Approach

Our introductory example, Caterpillar Inc., illustrates the need for a strategy evaluation approach that is focused on your potential customers. Now you have a stretch evaluation approach that explicitly addresses the opportunity you see in terms of customer requirements and the feasibility of stretching your current capabilities to achieve a successful market entry or to make the entry you are managing successful. You have a way to think about how you will capitalize on the capabilities and knowledge you have, and how to use them to satisfy the demands of your new customers.

The knowing corporation evaluates its business plan

early in the game. First, test whether you have the process capabilities and the knowledge, that is, the functional, technological, and management capabilities and competencies to serve your current customers' needs and the needs of any new customers. It is a practical way of addressing the question, How can you extend or stretch from your current resource base into a new market? This step is best taken before you worry about capital and other constraints. If the stretch vision seems feasible from the 3C perspective, you can assess the capital required and get excited about the probable return and your own rewards.

It is a relatively fast systems-level test for any business plan, including one that is already in progress. It will save a lot of effort, which might otherwise be wasted on detailing plans that just cannot fly. If you follow this approach and balance your resources against the target customers' needs before you leap, you will have fewer regrets and disappointments.

If the strategic leap has already been made and you are in the thick of it, fighting for your life, capitalize on what you have learned about stretching without breaking. For example, identify what you have learned about the market and your competitiveness, lift the collective awareness of any capability or knowledge gaps into high relief, and decide what resources are needed and what else needs to be done.

Swimming with the tide is easier than fighting it. Riding the waves of change is difficult but still easier than fighting them. Similarly, making time a friend rather than an enemy is always prudent—trying to win markets too fast can be a mistake, as Lincoln learned. Use this approach to negotiate for an appropriate timetable. Artful management teams will deliberately use the momentum and trends of the environment to multiply their company's market impact, buy time, and mitigate its risk exposure.

Some gaps and risks can be closed through reliance on

select enterprise partners, as we described in Chapter 3, and others by making your own internal investments in processes and competencies. Finally, if key gaps and risks seem to be unacceptable, you may be able to reshape your future strategy to limit the stretch required.

Conclusion

As Lincoln's losses proved while the knowledge economy is still taking shape, successful companies must deliberately invest time and effort in exploring and then entering new markets. Careful attempts to understand strategic stretch are most needed when early results are ambiguous and the competitive pressure to do something is high. Such situations require serious judgment, time, and effort. The future of your enterprise is put at risk whenever it is committed to a stretch initiative that exceeds its resources.

Feasible plans emerge when the explicit risks of venturing forth from your current competitive position are apparent. Identifying these risks allows you to reshape your commitments so that you only commit to what you and your partners can respectively afford—corporately and, of course, personally. When risks abound, the important characteristic of good management is to select those risks that you will take and to design controls that will quickly alert you to your own successes or problems. Then, what is needed is a will to manage, coupled with approaches for identifying causes of problems and finding better strategies as situations change. Chapter 5 will show you how to enhance your longer-term prospects for success by planning to manage risk rather than confronting it after the fact.

5
Managing Stretch Risks

When Walt Disney's original vision for an animated film business was rejected by prospective investors, the experience shaped his lifelong business philosophy. Later, Disney said that he knew he had a good idea when ten people whose judgment he respected said, "No. It won't work." His subsequent actions were based on his contrary view of what ten no votes meant. He believed that if you really understood why people rejected it, and eliminated the obstacles one by one, you would not only have a winner but an uncontested winner. There would be no competition, Disney argued, because if any of his ten people took his idea and presented it to another group of ten reasonable people, they would see the same obstacles and say no, too. The difference was, of course, that in his eyes, he would be the only one to stretch past the obstacles and seize the opportunity.

No doubt you have colleagues whose specialty is finding obstacles rather than thinking past them. To paraphrase a slogan from the 1960s: If you are not part of the solution, you are part of the problem. But a good solution is not mindless of the risks involved.

Evaluating Risk

The notion of risk may be more familiar to you with respect to financial investment than for matters of strategic direction. When large amounts of money are at risk, managers make considerable effort to secure their interests. In the heyday of the leveraged buyout (LBO) business of the 1980s, for example, prices paid for businesses rose from less than book value to several times book value. But while companies like Georgia Pacific spun off former divisions as independent "management-owned" organizations like Georgia Gulf, which had assets worth twenty times its equity, they were careful that the risks being taken were almost exclusively financial. Everyone involved, including the debt holders, made certain that the LBO target faced limited business risk by ensuring that it had the capabilities to compete out of the gate and the competencies to survive and renew itself. They recognized that the new company could carry either business or financial risk, but not both. To get the price they wanted for the business being sold—that is, to carry a highly leveraged capital structure—the business had to be competitively sound.

In the case of Georgia Gulf, its former parent, Georgia Pacific, contracted on a "take or pay" basis for an amount roughly equal to Georgia Gulf's breakeven load in its core product line, which made the financial arrangement more secure. Additionally, before the spin-off, Georgia Pacific had acquired several downstream businesses that were made part of the new Georgia Gulf. This was to ensure that Georgia Gulf had the competencies, customer relationships, and process capabilities in place to survive as a downstream player. For example, it had the manufacturing capacity and a cost position to ensure its competitive advantage for some years to come—enough time to shift its capital structure to normal and get the debt holders out with a profit.

In stretch initiatives where the point is to commit no additional capital, there are no outsiders, such as Georgia Gulf's lenders, to ask questions and force management to think about business risk. If the stretch initiative does not require formal internal financial approval, such as the capital review normally conducted by the CFO's office, a successful company may simply venture forth casually and meet unexpected problems that bring it to the brink of disaster. However, a knowing corporation will not do this because it will always want to know the risks that may lie ahead.

So, in this spirit of the knowing corporation, we will identify the questions you need to ask to know which risks you will face if you stretch toward a new opportunity. We call this approach the stretch test. The objective is to help you become an informed player in the evaluation and implementation phases of any stretch initiative you are involved with. The approach is shaped by Disney's insight that the best way to stretch is to identify the risks and obstacles you will face and then work to eliminate, bypass, shift, share, overcome, or control them if the opportunity you are stretching toward is large enough. We assume here that you have already determined that a particular opportunity is almost feasible at the 3C level but still carries some risk because of missing but needed capabilities and competencies.

Not Looking before You Leap

Let us begin with an example of what can happen when a company jumps to a new stretch strategy without enough prior consideration. One of Europe's greatest retail industry successes in the 1980s and early 1990s was Laura Ashley. Its success was due, in part, to a global stretch initiative where the company plunged into the U.S. market from its U.K. base. In 1999, after years of losses, it finally sold its North American business, about 40 percent of the firm's total turnover, for one dollar and exited this market. The trouble could be traced to Laura Ashley's being too confident to review the risks of its global stretch initiatives. They gave no signs of learning needed lessons from their early results.

Shortly before its collapse, Laura Ashley was aggressively attempting to boost sales on multiple fronts. Management was doing everything it could to leverage its brand name and get back into the black to boost its stock price. Figure 5-1 shows some key characteristics of Laura Ashley's geographic markets: its established U.K. market and its diversification targets close by in Europe, and, further afield, the United States. Simultaneously, with its geographic initiatives, the company also ventured from its established fabrics and upholstered furniture base in the United Kingdom into the fast-paced fashion markets and mail-order business for all its geographic markets. Figure 5-2 highlights what seem to be critical differences across these distinct product markets, for example, average transaction size, inventory turns, inventory risk, and fashion risk.

Unfortunately, it seems, Laura Ashley did not appreciate that its markets, both geographic and product-based, were very different from each other. Customers in each may have shared a liking for Laura Ashley's classic English country-floral look, but the dynamics and risks of each market required quite different information and control

Figure 5-1. Laura Ashley's market differences: geographic markets.

U.K. Market	U.S. Market	European Market
People will queue. Staff is experienced. Supply lines are short.	People will wait longer in the South and West. Staff is usually part-time, and experience is rare. Supply lines from United Kingdom are long.	How many Anglophiles live in France and the Maldives?

Figure 5-2. Laura Ashley's market differences: product markets.

Furniture	Garments	Mail Order
Big Ticket	Smaller Ticket	Mixed Product Line
Slow turn—20 percent annually	Fast turn, even faster than competitors'	Orders and payments before mfg.
Slow user—replacement cycle	Fast replacement cycle separates in United States	Could promotional value be important?
Customers likely expect to wait	Customers will not wait	Short waits are OK
Risk: Moderate	Fashion risks high, risk of inventory obsolescence high	Risk in supply and fulfillment controls needed on partners
Experienced staff important	Experience less necessary	No experience in servicing customers at a distance
Supply lines are delayed	Supply is seasonal	Supply must be responsive

systems because they operated at different speeds and they subjected the company to different risks.

Complications due to product-market differences were compounded by geographic differences and competency gaps within the company. Figure 5-3 suggests the increased complexity that Laura Ashley's constantly changing management teams had to contend with. For example, because the company was set up to operate in the relatively sedate European furniture market, its fulfillment processes were not synchronized with the higher-risk U.S. market. While the traditional European market was dominated by furniture sales, the U.S. market was fashion-conscious, thus creating the need for different service standards across the geographic regions. Furthermore, there were different buying cycles and issues of customer loyalty

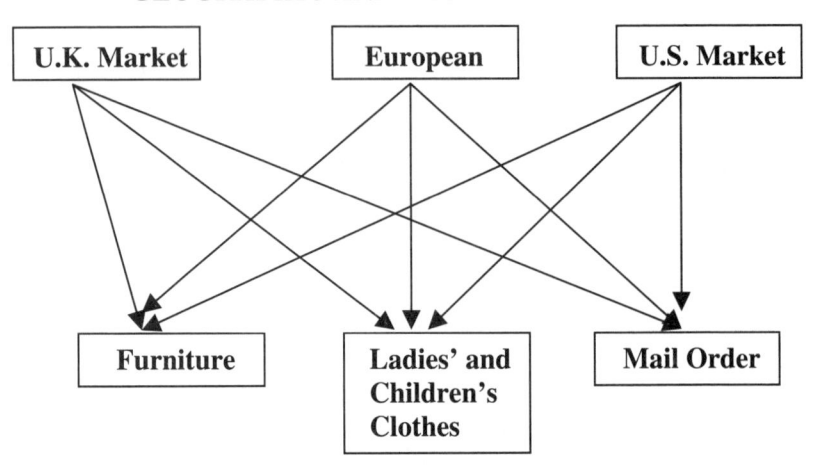

Figure 5-3. Laura Ashley's complex ambition.
GEOGRAPHIC AND PRODUCT MARKETS

```
┌─────────────┐    ┌─────────────┐    ┌─────────────┐
│ U.K. Market │    │  European   │    │ U.S. Market │
└─────────────┘    └─────────────┘    └─────────────┘

┌─────────────┐    ┌─────────────┐    ┌─────────────┐
│  Furniture  │    │ Ladies' and │    │  Mail Order │
│             │    │ Children's  │    │             │
│             │    │   Clothes   │    │             │
└─────────────┘    └─────────────┘    └─────────────┘
```

due to varying tolerance of product shortages or delivery failures.

Laura Ashley stretched, apparently without adequately recognizing these differences, suggesting that the organization lacked the competencies needed to manage its increasingly diverse enterprise. The company lacked the know-how to appreciate the differences that developed across their markets, especially the vulnerability of their U.S. business to a shift in fashion. They either did not identify the capabilities they needed to win in the United States, or they failed to appreciate that in the U.S. they would have to win over and over again, season by season, because these new customers had not made the types of purchases that increased the likelihood that they would return. This was in contrast to the U.K. market, where expensive upholstered furniture and drapery purchases essentially created a customer lock-in. Not seeing such differences between markets is consistent with Laura Ashley's creation of global supply lines that were out of synch with market-speed requirements, and control systems that provided poor information for decisions.

The root cause of the problem, we believe, is that Laura Ashley lacked local market competencies, despite its strong brand management and general marketing savvy. Furthermore, multimarket winners usually focus on one particular stretch at a time, to limit their risk exposure. Success in one market is rarely easy to replicate elsewhere, without either experienced staff or some lessons in the school of hard knocks. The difficulty of leaping in with little thought is that the school of hard knocks charges large fees. Laura Ashley executives learned this lesson too late.

In every stretch situation, management teams have to address the risks from expanding off the base of their existing capabilities and competencies. Hence, making the effort to evaluate a stretch strategy, both up front and again from the trenches along the way, is worthwhile. Senior management needs to be able to make a complete evaluation up front, preferably with the operating managers who are responsible for executing that strategy.

Prudent managers do not bet their company unless their backs are against the wall. Prudence means acting ahead of need, and recognizing the demands of your ambition and your company's real constraints before committing to act. Then it is great to be entrepreneurial like Disney, working to add value by levering the new knowledge to differentiate your business from the competition.

Looking before You Leap

To illustrate a more careful stretch initiative, and the types of incisive resource deployments that can lead to a highly advantaged competitive position, we turn to Otis Elevator's European experience. Otis not only had a good strategy, it made choices about executing the strategy that allowed it to manage its risks.

The Strategic Stretch at Otis

Some years ago, the European elevator industry restructured when Otis stretched from its traditional and prestigious high-rise A-class markets to enter the previously overlooked, but larger, B-class markets for three- and four-floor elevators. This strategy represented a significant stretch for Otis into a new category of customer, new products, and new services. As you will see, they moved with deliberate care into what could have been a risky venture. By expanding into the then-unserved (by Otis and the other A-class manufacturers) B-class market, Otis built a Pan-European manufacturing and service organization that had outstanding capabilities, wider scope, and lower-cost service than any of its competitors.

Otis's management realized that its market position was vulnerable, perhaps to a Japanese entry into a market segment at the bottom of the elevator market in the then-emerging European Economic Community (EEC). Perceiving this risk, Otis's European management was determined to preempt this from happening by moving into the gap itself. It resolved to move aggressively and to build advantage with a deliberate stretch strategy that would tap the company's existing engineering and manufacturing competencies and build upon their existing post-sales service capabilities. The strategy was to expand the service business as fast as possible and make it a cash cow. Although they were a division of the world's leading elevator manufacturer, Otis Europe had to contend with a very real constraint—they had to fund themselves, and stay in the black. There would be no funding from corporate headquarters.

How Otis Managed Its Risks

Otis Europe intentionally limited its risks by moving slowly and selectively intensifying the pressures it put on the competition. Recognizing that Germany was the key market in Europe, they entered the German B-class market, knowing that they would be competing against small regional companies that had never before contested a market with a better-capitalized, multinational, A-class supplier.

Otis's expansion required no new partnerships or alliances because it already had the basic process capabilities and organizational competencies it needed. But it had to become cost-competitive against its regional competition. Otis decided to standardize the design of its B-class elevators prior to its entry into the market. This decision narrowed the product scope and allowed Otis to control a critical risk element by simplifying the manufacturing for its new product line. The acceleration of its field-based learning about elevator assembly and installation was expected to lower its service inventory investments in the long haul. In total, Otis's standardization decision was perfectly consistent with its development of a superior order fulfillment process that was capable of operating at higher conformance levels than the old system it replaced.

Another potential source of risk to Otis in this venture was time. It was uncertain how long it would take to make Otis's presence felt in this new B-class elevator marketplace and reach needed economies of scale. To shorten the transition and to help it break into the market, many observers believe that Otis actually priced below manufacturing costs to promote the sales of its new products. Later, it acquired several small companies, along with their sales forces and service inventories. These were moves that appear to have accelerated the development of Otis's large base of installed elevators in the B-market. Remember, the plan was to quickly grow the service business to ensure success with more extensive service capabilities, higher service capacity utilization, and lower service prices.

The major B-market competition tried to compete by offering better credit terms rather than by changing any of their process capabilities. And, because the competition failed to shift their fulfillment processes to Otis's model, Otis enjoyed a perceived advantage in the market, which further strengthened their future business for a time. Finally, Otis's advantaged service position, in turn, contributed the funds that capitalized a still faster rate of growth in the B markets, and then, ultimately, the A-class markets in Europe.

One reason for the competition's slow response was that as Otis built share in the B product and service markets, it appeared to be losing money on manufacturing and installation. But, unnoticed by the competition, Otis was earning substantial expanding profits on service. Its competitive advantage was building although its corporate-level profits were barely holding steady.

Otis's market entry was well controlled, and it seems likely that they held future B elevator prices at no more than a few dollars under their current manufacturing cost as they drove costs down. Ultimately, Otis succeeded in converting the whole industry to its strategy. But by then, Otis was in the leading and most profitable position due to its expanded service revenues, low overhead, standardized product lines, rationalized production facilities, and low manufacturing and installation costs. This was a very robust strategy. It positioned Otis as the advantaged supplier in its markets in every economic scenario. In bad times, it had the lowest cost and so the lowest prices; in good times, standardization facilitated on-schedule delivery when delivery really counted to its customers; and, at all times, low-priced reliable service fueled higher levels of customer satisfaction.

Otis clearly incorporated a wide range of stretch factors in its strategic plan. From the beginning, working off its own global management competencies, Otis intended to take full advantage of the opportunities offered by shifting government policies within the EEC to create the first Pan-European elevator company. Then, they decided to focus their plans to achieve the realizable scale economies, and added new capabilities to enter service at continental versus local scale. They executed their strategy one step at a time over ten years. Along the way, demanding performance standards and high levels of accountability, enforced by the self-funding decision, pressured the fulfillment processes to learn and develop new competencies that, in turn, refined the company's manufacturing capabilities. Otis had a vision, a self-funding stretch strategy to realize that vision, and the will to execute its strategy because management fostered accountability to maintain control.

The Importance of Questions

Depending upon when one evaluated Otis's strategy—upfront, along the way, or after the fact one might have had less or more confidence in the strategy. However, when you are evaluating strategies partway through the game, be cautious when confronted by an isolated positive or negative result. If the meaning of a result is uncertain, ask "Why?" five times to get to the bottom of things as Taiichi Ohno, Toyota's own manufacturing guru and reformer, once counseled. Otis's apparent manufacturing losses and slow profit growth created early doubts about the wisdom of its strategy, but these results masked its increased market share, vital service organization, lower manufacturing costs, and, most importantly, an increasingly robust competitive position. Otis's competitors who focused on single measures of performance were misled, while Otis's board saw the full pattern of results and sustained its stretch effort.

Success is founded in theories, hunches, and insights that have been tested by first asking and then answering important questions. You need information, market knowledge, and physical and management resources to allow you to push on. You need results to bolster confidence both within the ranks and above you for support. If you are in charge of a function or business process in a business unit that is stretching, you will have to determine how to control the action and limit your corporate and personal risk exposure to what you can afford. In the Otis situation, the constrained capital situation imposed by the parent company and its accountability system forced the European management team to stretch with care.

Facing a Harsh Reality: The Inevitability of Risk

How can we learn from the very different experiences of Laura Ashley and Otis? The point of stretching further is to seize new and larger opportunities and to garner their rewards, as Laura Ashley attempted and Otis won. You pay the price of risk to gain advantage. But the price of risk can be controlled if your organization learns to anticipate its elements and how they might successfully be managed.

As you stretch and become more venturesome, the stakes will rise, so there is a growing need to prudently assess the risks that you are likely to experience. The more new process capabilities you need, the riskier the venture could be. When you also need new organizational competencies, the risks rise again. As the risks increase, you have to decide which risks to take and which are unaffordable. Although you cannot escape risk, you can choose the risks to take. Care is needed because the risks that you fail to identify will cause most of your future problems.

The major risks associated with no change should be apparent after the 3C assessment that you learned in Chapter 3. Less apparent, however, may be your exposure to new risks from the proposed stretch itself. For example, holding low inventories brings the risk of supply delays in the order fulfillment process, but holding large inventories is, in itself, a risky action if technology is likely to shift or if input prices fall. Similarly, while increased scale reduces the risk of cost competition, this strategy may bring new risks of reduced supply responsiveness to some existing customers.

As you identify the explicit risks of your stretch initiative one by one, explore what you can do to manage them. For example, the specific management controls you choose to put in place will allow you to determine, early on, whether you are succeeding or getting into trouble. The purpose of the controls is to produce information to inform your subsequent actions and reactions and to focus your managerial energy and commitment on matters that count.

Another strategy, when you conclude that a risk is unaffordable, is to seek other qualified organizations that might take them for you, for example, for a fee, through a contract or collaborative partnership, or a share of the enterprise you are creating. But, as you do so, again remember the basic principle that a decision to avoid one risk means accepting the costs of another. Consider the risk of contracting out to leverage competencies controlled by others—for example, switching from manufacturing in its own factory to contract manufacturing. In this circumstance, a hidden risk is hollowing out. In the 1980s, for example, U.S. companies that relied upon offshore manufacturing were labeled hollow. Although the image of being hollowed-out formerly referred only to the lack of a production capability, now it extends beyond the manufacturing function into the realms of market sensing, building customer loyalty, service, and product design and development, among others.

Managers who overlook the future value of their competencies when they contract out may find themselves with a hollowed-out organization that lacks the key knowledge and expertise to adapt and prosper. Therefore, companies need internal manufacturing competencies to help shape their vision of what can be, and to successfully regulate their manufacturing contracts. If those organizational competencies are not built new and perhaps greater, business risks will arise later on. So, even when widespread contracting out appears to be a sensible downsizing step before drastically cutting personnel, ask the new question about risk: Are we downsizing to the point of risking the loss of organizational competencies that will cripple our future if they are not rebuilt? Hollowing out can be an unacceptably high price of stretching through badly structured contracts—a price appreciated too late if the original stretch evaluation was incomplete.

Unfortunately, the most significant costs of competency gaps are fully revealed only in the future. Such costs must be estimated in advance, largely in terms of the value of lost opportunities if the company fails to close these gaps by acquiring the necessary organizational competencies. Closing competency gaps will, of course, have a cost—either the investments to build them internally or the commitment to an expense stream for renting them from partners or contractors.

You can only stretch if you are prepared to change, which requires overcoming the tendency to avoid the risk of change by appreciating the risk of not changing. The risks you take and the ways you measure your organization's performance interact to either foster adaptive behavior or shackle your organization to its past. This big question of strategic risk preference, mapped in Figure 5-4, measured against the focus of your organizational performance measurement system may be something your management team needs to become aware of and comfortable with.

One error that is common among older, well-established companies is believing your strategy is right when it is not. Mark Twain put it something like this: "It ain't what I knowed that done me in, but what I knowed that just wasn't so." These companies accept the risk of not

Figure 5-4. Strategic choices—conscious or unconscious.

FOCUS OF PERFORMANCE MEASUREMENT SYSTEM

	Internal & Short-Term		External & Long-Term
Insufficient Change	Older Long Successful Companies	Older Service Companies	Monopoly Holders
Too Much Change	Young Management Teams in Old Companies	Modern Service Companies	Fast-Paced Industry Leaders

STRATEGIC RISK ACCEPTED

changing their business strategy. They choose not to stretch, and, as a result, forgo the opportunity to learn in zones beyond their current businesses. They subject themselves to the risk of failing to adapt in a timely way, because they are under the false impression that change is unwarranted. The alternative error, incurred by venturesome organizations, is believing your strategy is wrong when it is not. At an extreme, such a company would try to avoid the risk of not changing by changing constantly. The downside here is burdening the organization with the costs and confusion of unwarranted change and fighting legitimate resistance to ill-considered change.

The alternative to these two extremes is to be prudent and to avoid either of these two blinding biases. Admit that there are always good reasons for sticking with an old profitable strategy and for changing strategies in a sensible way. And, plan to sort out what you should do next by grounding your plans in a knowledge-managed decision process that lets you make a good strategic choice after a rapid but full and systematic consideration of its potential risks and rewards.

Thus, when you stretch, know what you are taking on and why. What to do depends on the company and its peculiar circumstances. Companies can limit the likelihood of "no change" errors by lengthening their performance horizons, using more criteria to evaluate their situations and strategies, and occasionally trying to prove to themselves that their current theory of the business is *not* valid. Companies can limit the likelihood of "always change" errors by deliberate stretching in ways that limit the commitment to change, while offering learning potential from ongoing reviews of lessons learned. In the end, however, the harsh reality is that some risk is inevitable.

When your company's performance measurement system is focused on internally defined short-term results, the dire consequences of your strategic risk preference are likely to be exacerbated. Established companies lagging in today's economy, as well as failing e-commerce start-ups, generally fall into this category. In contrast, the leaders of the old and new economies alike seem to not only take the risks they do deliberately and prudently, but do so because their measures of success are defined in terms of the market and their customers' long-term interests. Fast-paced industry leaders seem to be companies that are externally focused and constantly exploring new opportunities.

Making Stretch Feasible

Whenever you have determined—using the approach presented in Chapter 4—that a stretch plan is almost feasible rather than fully feasible in its 3C assessment, it is time for full risk assessment. The objective is to complete a comprehensive assessment of all risks well before resources are committed. Becoming aware of the risks ahead will allow you to choose while there is time to think and shape your strategic commitments and timing, and, therefore, to help preserve your ability to be self-determining.

Here, then, is a brief but comprehensive list of factors for your consideration:

- Market attractiveness and resource feasibility
- Competitive advantage and competitive surprise
- External stakeholder constraints
- Internal stakeholder constraints

The first three categories deal with the knowledge and judgment needed to create the case that your stretch plan is fundamentally feasible, affordable, and likely to be rewarding. The fourth category, internal stakeholder constraints, recognizes that plans need both commitment and support from within the company. Without support, the plan is likely to be unsustainable.

Your objective here is not to minimize aggregate risk, but rather to identify its separate components and adopt a risk management posture that serves your company or business unit. This means selecting which risks to take, which to avoid entirely, and which to farm out. You have to weigh the payoff from carrying a particular risk yourself against its costs. Clearly, there is a lot to be done.

To get organized and ensure that you complete the task, you will want to have some structure to guide you. Use Figure 5-5 as a template for collecting what is known, your judgments, and the risks that need to be managed. The process is to work across the table from left to right, moving across the columns and then down, row by row, summarizing the way you and your management team see each factor listed in the left-hand column impacting your strategy by adding risk. Finally, you access the total pattern of your individual assessments and decide what to do. We will begin with the first category, opportunity, and discuss its attractiveness and feasibility.

Market Attractiveness and Resource Feasibility—the 3Cs

Assuming that you already have a good handle on customers, capabilities, and competencies for your new strategy and know where you may be at risk along those dimensions, we will simply use this part of the table to set up all the later work. Start with the first row of Figure 5-5, the target customer. Summarize the current situation, as you see it, in column 1 by defining the opportunity available to your company along with your prospective customers' key performance expectations. List the market risks you see in column 2. Next, identify the principal elements of the stretch strategy in column 3. Try to be explicit about the

Figure 5-5. Assessing stretch risk.

Knowledge Content	Situation at Present (1)	Current Risks Faced (2)	Stretch Objective (3)	Advantage to Be Gained (4)	Implementation Risks (5)	Action to Control Risk (6)	Probability of Success (Go/No) (7)
Customers							
Capabilities							
Competencies							
Competition							
Unserved Customer							
Capital and Contracts							
Country and Currency							
Coalitions							
CEO							

advantage to be gained by stretching to the new market in column 4. Then, identify the new customer-linked risks associated with this effort in column 5. Follow up in column 6 by identifying enhancements to the strategy that you could use to reduce all these risks; for example, actions you could take to limit these risks or to otherwise control your risk exposure should you decide to proceed. Finally, in column 7, simply record your final assessment of the knowledge and judgments recorded in this row with a go or no decision. It is a decision based on consideration of this one risk factor (row) only—a judgment that the probability of success is high enough to warrant a go or low enough to say no.

Repeat the process for capabilities, and, then, for competencies to get the whole record in one place. This will help you to make your total assessment of the situation, both personally and corporately. What will determine the ultimate commit decision is the overall pattern of go/no judgments, and your ability to manage the risks you identify, rather than a decision based on any single factor. When you use this approach, you will be able to make more informed judgments about the risks ahead, why they are worth taking, and the controls you might use to ameliorate them. Of course, insights stem not from the list, but from the process set up to identify and weight them.

Competitive Advantage and Competitive Surprise

The second set of risk factors includes competition and the ever-shifting unserved market—often the source of unpleasant surprises. First, we will deal with competition in the target market because stretching is a market entry strategy and, in most situations, there is very likely competition already in place. Who they are and how they compete can be summarized in column 1. Work across the other columns. What risks to you do your competitors impose now?

What are you trying to achieve with respect to them—will you be taking market share, for example, by trying to woo their high-volume customers? What will be the basis of your advantage? What risks are you going to take as you enter? How could you be surprised, either happily or to your chagrin or regret? What data will you need to keep on top of the situation and know which way the cookie is going to crumble? What will you do if things go awry—that is, what is your control strategy? On balance, is the competition and your relative advantage strong enough to justify a go decision?

Next, move down a row and consider the unserved markets. Quite often new competition or new opportunities emerge in customer segments that you decided to stay out of long ago—segments of your current market that you have deliberately ignored and are likely to ignore in the future, as well as apparently unattractive segments of your target market. What is happening within them? Are any threats emerging? Could you be surprised? Is the opportunity in them changing? Should your objective for this segment change, for defensive or other reasons? Can you monitor the situation better? Is it worth the effort? Will change there impact your stretch initiative and threaten it in some way, or could it help you win? Again, on balance, is the force with you or not? Will you enjoy a competitive advantage?

External Stakeholder Constraints

Now turn to external constraints. Move down another row and assess how much capital is needed to sustain the stretch, and whether any incremental investments are required. Is the extra funding needed? What will it cost, and will there be strings attached? Will supply contracts cut capital needs and risk, and how might such contracts be managed to reduce your capital at risk while protecting your competencies and long-run future? What control and coordination risks would you take on to manage your supply chain during the stretch?

Then, identify how governments, possibly your local communities, state and federal authorities, nation states across the world, or even action groups, could either constrain or support your initiative. What costs need to be considered along with these external influences? For example, with respect to the cost of access to particular countries, learn whether the host governments require local equity ownership or complementary investments to boost national employment, and whether there are special tax considerations if higher-value work is included in your entry proposal. Determine also, especially if you have not had prior experience doing business in that country, what its corruption index is. Assess the likelihood that you will be able to deal with local corruption yet be in compliance with applicable laws and our own corporate ethical standards.

If you are considering a big stretch toward becoming more global, make an effort to identify the order of magnitude of your probable additional exposure to currency shifts. Will currency shifts impact revenue, income, assets, or debt? How can you protect the enterprise from the unexpected with hedges and futures contracts and the like? Whether the enterprise is global in scope or not, you might also need to consider the importance of community support, services, and licensing practices to your success.

Internal Stakeholder Constraints

So far, the knowledge being assembled is being structured into a case for a commitment to the stretch initiative or its rejection. At this point, if your stretch test is building toward a go decision, you or some other manager will have to sell it up into the organization and win support for the new strategy. Therefore, you should assess the likelihood that this can be successfully accomplished at this time. After all, the lack of some critical element of internal commitment can offer enough risk to make an otherwise sound strategy infeasible. So you will want to question the variety and magnitude of internal stakeholder constraints upon the strategy being considered. What inside leaders need to be involved? Whose commitment is essential? Who will support you and why? At what price, and to what effect? Can you form a coalition with them to get things moving forward? How can they work together to test their sense of the market and alternative strategies, and to learn how to improve them before seeking a corporate commitment? How can you trigger a timely corporate commitment? Can it be done now? And, should you make the effort now, or will the company be better served by a postponement?

And, finally, in the last row, deal with the situation from the CEO's point of view. Chief executive officers represent the formal face of the corporate enterprise, typically have a veto on plans, and can provide powerful support when they are convinced of the merits of a proposal. But CEOs are trapped by the organization's need for continuity, and can not test new directions without risking confusion across the organization. Hence, because the CEO's public and formal support triggers a corporate-wide commitment, this factor is always of great competitive significance. The coalition working to implement the strategy needs to have answers to the CEO's questions, and they need to have a convincing case for change. Do you believe that this objective is reasonable in the context of your stretch strategy?

A Go or No-Go Decision

Once all the relevant knowledge has been gathered and evaluated row by row, you are ready to complete the stretch test by sizing up the whole situation. Consider the total pattern of constraints and risks. Will your controls limit the dangers raised? Are the constraints or risks still too great? Exactly what factors are still troublesome? Identify the limiting risks and overall costs. Will developing a key partnership with another company solve these problems? After reviewing your stretch strategy on each factor, decide whether the effort is worth the time, cost, and risk compared to the potential advantage to be gained and the rewards to be had. This go/no-go overall assessment must, out of necessity, be highly subjective, but it will help move you toward a conclusion about your plan.

Ultimately, the decision of whether and how to proceed should be based on the pattern as a whole. Every positive assessment is a boost to confidence. Every negative is a stop-and-think-again signal. A preponderance of positive signals means go ahead, but watch carefully for any change-direction signals in the negative test areas. A majority of negatives means that you should back off or go back to the drawing board to rework the problem or opportunity, again and again, until you find a winning way.

This stretch test is a structured approach to dealing with issues at the business—or even multibusiness enterprise—level and is a way to ensure informed decision making. Different managers and specialists will have knowledge to contribute, sometimes explicit but often tacit, which should be shared and jointly considered. Your own knowledge base may be limited to only one of the factors that needs to be considered. But you can add value, along with the others, to this comprehensive knowledge management effort. The complexity and potential impact of your candidate strategy determine the factors that deserve the most attention and the level of effort that is appropriate. Being roughly correct in all your assessments relating to the proposed strategy is much more important than being precisely correct on some of them but having not considered others at all.

Using the Stretch Test: Hewlett-Packard Singapore

To give you a more tangible sense of how to apply the stretch test, consider a particular stretch strategy used by Hewlett-Packard (HP). During the 1990s, HP was busy restructuring and moving into new markets. Top management initiated some of the changes it made, but others were the outcomes of stretch programs directly initiated by its operating managers. One such strategy dealt with the timing, scope, and responsibility for HP's entry into the Japanese market for desktop printers. Initially conceived of by the management of a small HP factory in Singapore, the proposal was considered too difficult and risky for Singapore to attempt. Nevertheless, this business unit took up the challenge.

This factory had been founded many years earlier to make quality parts inexpensively, taking advantage of Singapore's low-cost labor. Then, consistent with Singapore's industrial development policies, HP had converted this plant from making parts to assembling products such as calculators, keyboards, solid state displays, and integrated circuits. And, although it had its own manufacturing capacity, Singapore became highly competent at component procurement and contracted with other experienced manufacturers for parts, and with these suppliers, managed the cost out of its products.

Despite the lack of corporate support for its proposed stretch initiative, the local management team in Singapore saw the situation as "needing rework." They were determined to seize the opportunity to stretch into the Japanese market despite the difficulties. Considering market attractiveness and competition, for example, they argued the Japanese market was important because of the size of the opportunity on the one hand, and, on the other, their belief that to compete effectively against HP's Japanese rivals, it would have to face them on their home ground. Hence, opportunity and defense justified some form of entry.

Unfortunately, their assessment of the stretch needed to serve the Japanese customer was greater than Singapore could attempt alone. Neither HP Singapore, nor HP corporate headquarters, had competencies in marketing their products to the Japanese. Furthermore, it seemed likely that a successful entry would require a product line tailored to Japanese performance expectations. Unfortunately, Singapore had no design capability and limited design competence, although it was clear that product redesign would be necessary for a highly successful product introduction in Japan.

Limited market research had revealed that Japanese buyers would welcome the relatively unknown HP, but only if the company could match their needs. To win, HP would need to reduce the size of its printers because space is expensive in Japan, cut costs and prices, hold quality high, print Japanese characters, and be suitable for the home production of the many seasonal postcards the Japanese exchanged with each other throughout the year since the competitors' products could print these cards.

Despite the fact that HP's inkjet printers could not meet any of these specifications at the time, rather than being deterred from their ambition, Singapore took full advantage of ongoing HP programs to widen its capabilities and to develop the competencies needed to support them. One of its strategies was to step up to the plate to do more when some other HP unit had a problem. Also stimulating its efforts was the payoff enhancement that Singapore's tax incentives gave to companies that increased value-adding activities in Singapore and added high-wage jobs dealing with technology and product development. The government of Singapore was likely to be in favor of its initiative and would make corporate friends at HP simply by being helpful—the foundation for later coalitions for change.

As HP Singapore's functional competencies grew because of its wider role in other HP projects, and as its capabilities expanded along with those of its Singapore-based and Malaysian suppliers, it was also positioning the company for a Japanese market entry. Even though it still lacked marketing competencies and had no order acquisition process in Japan, it was able to learn more about the target market by collaborating with a small Yokogawa-HP joint venture sales office in Japan.

The analysis of this stretch venture came down to a tough decision: either enter quickly, but not with a truly new product designed to fully meet the expressed needs of the Japanese buyer, or wait. Principal among the risks of waiting was that Japanese competitors would probably continue to encroach upon HP's markets in the United States, in part because they were being unchallenged in their own domestic market.

This complex situation could reasonably lead to go or no-go decisions by HP's Singapore and corporate management, depending not only on their assessment of the risks identified but on their sense of how much risk HP could afford and how much learning was necessary to win in Japan. But, by putting all the risks on the table and assessing their costs versus the benefits of learning the market and beginning to make their presence felt in Japan, fast entry was viewed as a step toward a more vital future. It is exactly the type of debate and decision the stretch test, as summarized in Figure 5-5, is intended to facilitate.

What possibly tipped the balance in favor of a go decision in this situation was HP's huge war chest of several billion underutilized dollars and the willingness of the corporation's top management team to promote stretch initiatives across the company in pursuit of growth on a global basis. Because Singapore had prepared for this stretch initiative for several years, and because it was prepared to start small and expand with success, it ultimately won the go-ahead. Its early success was circumscribed as expected, but with a beachhead established, HP was soon able to deliver a competitive product and widen its head-to-head competition with the Japanese across the globe.

Conclusion

Stretching is one positive step toward new opportunities and new strategies. But stretching without breaking calls for a comprehensive assessment of the risks likely to be faced, and the strategies for controlling those risks. The stretch test presented here is driven by questions and places a premium on knowledge management across a wide set of strategic factors. The questions presented in this chapter signal what you need to know. They will help your company structure the evaluation so that your collective knowledge can be used to identify the important risks you will face before you commit to any stretch strategy.

Because the range of issues likely to be faced is wide, a set of managers, drawn from all the key business functions and processes, should participate in the stretch assessment. No one person should expect to have all of the answers. In the stretch zone, the collective past experience and available external information is necessarily going to be inadequate to remove all risk. What you can do, however, is identify the risks you will be taking, develop appropriate controls for them, and know you need to be alert to sense surprise.

Operating managers in a knowing corporation are aware of their company's explicit objectives, and performance targets over time. This helps them determine when and where to intervene as their company positions itself to manage the risks that have been identified in advance. By participating in this strategy evaluation process, they become more valued members of the company's leadership team, with responsibility for some aspect of strategic stretch.

6

Experimenting to Build Competencies

Astonishing changes have been made to our business models during recent years. Barnes & Noble, a leading bookstore chain, decided to embrace the Internet in response to the huge success of the virtual store created by Amazon.com, a start-up pioneer in e-commerce. They formed a new entity, a Web-based venture called Barnesandnoble.com, which had to quickly develop the competency to acquire orders and provide information in a manner that was new to them. Soon after, Amazon.com sought to secure its industry position by taking on the new challenges of inventory management as it moved from being merely an order-taker to a full service sales, warehouse, and distribution management company.

Both of these companies needed to know how to build particular organizational competencies that were currently missing, but were critical to the success of their new business models. Organizational competencies, or know-how, are the limiting resource when management decides it is time to change the business model or to venture well beyond established markets to find new opportunities. In such situations, especially when a new entrant shakes things up and threatens other companies' survival, current capabilities are not enough to ensure continued success. Similarly, the changes that subject your company to new and unfamiliar risks will require you to develop new competencies within the company. For example, when pursuing a new class of customers with few proven capabilities in place, you will need to simultaneously build knowledge of new products, services, and process technologies. You will also need to learn how to develop new market-sensing competencies so the company can reach its new customers at an advantage. But how will you gain such knowledge?

Specially selected new business activity becomes a natural test bed for new strategies and an incubator for building new competencies. Tests are important because their results will either support the new "theory of the business" or refute it. They will also shed light on the nature of the target market and help management to identify the capability and competency gaps it needs to close to win in its new markets. Having a competency incubator strategy is similarly important because competencies have to be acquired ahead of need, either through internal development or through new partnerships or joint ventures.

Whether you are a small or large player in your corporate hierarchy, there is a role for you to play when things change like this. And, you will play it better if you have a clear understanding of how knowledge is created by collecting data, structuring it to reveal its information content, and asking and answering questions. In this stretch zone, questions are catalysts for knowledge-building, which, in turn, is an essential attribute of an adaptive organization.

To become adaptive and move out from established markets, an organization must develop confidence in its own judgment. And the key to confidence is knowledge that is grounded in fact rather than guesswork. Because a knowing corporation is skilled in asking the right questions, it is constantly aware of the kinds of information that matters most to its future and, as we have seen in prior chapters, proceeds with dispatch to create knowledge from action.

Here, we present a dynamic approach to learning-from-action through experiments. Experiments can be used to explore the uncertainties you face at limited risk, and to help prepare your organization for its more aggressive stretch initiatives. The basic idea is that, rather than committing to a risky large-scale initiative, the corporation steps into the unknown with carefully considered limited-scope experiments to generate knowledge as to where additional investments will be required and whether such commitment is warranted. If properly designed and executed, such strategic experiments create new knowledge about the corporation's markets, proposed strategies, and process changes, and in their execution begin to develop new competencies. The broadest question for triggering such experiments is, Will our new business model work? Additional strategic questions of the type you might want to address in your own business are listed in Figure 6-1.

Figure 6-1. Typical questions for driving strategic experiments.

- What is the potential of a new market?
- How does a new customer group differ from those we are accustomed to serving?
- How might we achieve radically improved cost reductions?
- How can one of our core business functions, or business processes, become more effective?
- How might a new strategy, accompanied by a set of incremental additions to certain organizational competencies and process capabilities, affect performance?
- What performance improvements might we be able to expect from a new Web-based initiative?

What Are Business Experiments?

Business experiments designed to explore any of these types of questions are partial and tentative probes of the unknown. They should run parallel with your existing ongoing business operations. In most companies, they are conducted covertly, which is unfortunate since it means we hear little about them. Successes are usually proclaimed, but failures are often quickly and unceremoniously buried, without review to the cost of losing the potential of lessons learned. This state of affairs is antithetical to the knowing corporation, where experiments are opportunities to learn for its managers, no matter the outcome. However, be aware that managers who have tried to experiment openly have first had to convince their direct supervisors that "failures" warrant review—not to find the guilty or to punish the uninvolved—but to promote learning and to uncover new questions. It is a new perspective for many, and one that can be personally risky unless the company culture embraces the notion that long-run success is rarely won without some failures on the way. People have to appreciate that what counts is not their intermediate score, but the long-run victory.

Because many executives view open business experiments as being personally risky, experimentation is an underutilized strategy. Its underutilization means that most of the organization's best ideas are essentially untested, and management has little advance sense of the connections between new strategic initiatives and their likely outcomes. As you will see from the following examples, while some experiments can be tightly controlled and scientifically designed, others will be less controlled and designed more intuitively. They may even be intentionally biased to accelerate the learning process.

Most strategic experiments are sponsored by senior

management, with the intention of learning something new and then taking appropriate extraordinary action. This fact makes them different from prototypes or pilots, which—whether they deal with a product, a manufacturing plant, or a new marketing plan—are better understood from the start and are supposed to succeed because they have already benefited from the application of proven competencies. Strategic experiments are also different from efforts to improve a company's existing operations by applying shared learning about best practices within the company and strengthening alignment with current customers, which was discussed in Chapter 2.

Put another way, experiments are an opportunity for creating rather than simply transferring strategic knowledge. Thus, experiments are in the spirit of the observation—which was expressed by management scholars Nonaka and Takeuchi[1] and considerably earlier by Ackoff[2]—that managers have to create knowledge if they want to successfully create businesses.

Experiments precede new strategic commitments. They are launched to thoroughly explore a potential strategy's acknowledged and, perhaps, still unknown risks. Even when not scientifically controlled, such experiments can generate sufficient experience to guide future strategy formulation. When there are limited resource commitments and market exposure, they can be used to provide insights on the real options that can shape a company's future. By definition, experiments reduce risk, although they cannot affect underlying uncertainty.

A Learning-from-Action Experiment: Steuben

Although not recent, the case of Steuben Glass provides a good look at an experiment aimed at learning from action.

At one time Steuben, a subsidiary of Corning Glass, made a wide line of colored glass bowls, glasses, and ornamental pieces. Its salespeople sold these products to any retail outlet willing to carry them. At Steuben's peak, almost 3,000 outlets across the United States carried its products. Orders of any size were accepted, and Steuben would make minor product variations to please a particular store. Then, because of the setup costs of making one piece, Steuben usually made several copies, placing the remainder in inventory. During the Great Depression, Steuben became so unprofitable that Corning considered closing it.

In 1933, however, Corning decided to turn the business over to a new management team that was headed by Arthur A. Houghton, Jr. A member of Corning's founding family, Houghton graduated from Harvard University in 1929 and was already known as a patron of the arts. Houghton realized the company was selling handmade products to the mass market. He believed Steuben had the formula for the finest clear crystal in the world and that hand production offered advantages in design, craftsmanship, and quality. Houghton determined that under his management the company would emphasize these outstanding attributes. The question was, How?

Houghton's first move was to direct an extensive market test of his new business concept. He called it an *experiment*. After focusing on Steuben's best-selling styles, he decided to eliminate colors and make products in clear crystal only, raising prices so that each piece was profitable. He also experimented with limited distribution. Before the experiment, Steuben had three large and twenty small accounts in Boston. After careful consideration, Houghton chose the fine jeweler and art dealer Shreve, Crump, and Low—which is still located in Boston's upscale Back Bay—and offered it an exclusive dealership in the city. Shreve's was to agree, in turn, to display the glass by itself in a simple case without placards, to maintain posted prices, and to stress the qualities of the glass itself in its advertising, not their store's prestige. The rest of the U.S. distribution channel was left alone, thereby reducing the company's commitment to the new strategy and its risk.

During the next ten months, this one store sold more glass than all twenty-three of the company's preexisting Boston accounts had sold the year before. The record of Steuben's past sales in Boston was Houghton's primary benchmark, while the sales trend across the remainder of the United States was the control that provided more confidence about his conclusions. The result suggested that the new business strategy could be successful and became the platform for a transformational change in his small company.

Strategic Experiments: Science and Art

At Steuben, Arthur Houghton, Jr., experimented to make sense of a complex situation and to test some hunches. By calling his actions an experiment, Houghton signaled that he was prepared to fail, but was also set up to learn. And, he was artful since he seems to have stacked the deck to gain fast insights—an administrative characteristic of many strategic experiments that differentiates them from pure science. Because of this bias, some people reject the idea that Houghton experimented with limited distribution in Boston. They argue that he knew the city and saw it as the place where his new strategy would work—that he was unscientific.

Skilled managers should think otherwise and follow their own traditions, choosing when fully-fledged experimental design is warranted and when it is not. We have seen effective managers conduct lightly controlled, and even *biased* experiments, to gather the data that they need to convince others that it is time to change strategies. Used with skill, lightly controlled and biased experiments like Steuben's can be very effective change accelerators—recall that Houghton restricted his experiment to Boston.

Experiments may be intentionally biased to check intuition, provide fast results, and generate new insights while limiting risk, which are steps aimed at building the confidence to act. Consider how the Steuben experiment was biased. First, we suspect that Houghton chose Boston because he knew Boston, having been in college there. He probably also chose Boston because, being a smaller market than New York City, it represented a more affordable risk for Steuben, and himself. Moreover, because the wealthy patrons of the arts lived at least some of the year within the city, Houghton probably knew that Shreve's was where they shopped since he would have shopped there himself. Moreover, he designed his exclusive agreement to put Shreve's scarcest resources—its shelf space and advertising dollars—behind Steuben's product for the first time.

With these advantages, compared with its limited past marketing support, if the experiment failed, Houghton would know that his hunch about the power of exclusive limited distribution was clearly wrong. On the other hand, if it worked well, Houghton could use the results to convince retailers in larger cities, such as New York, to make similar commitments. Indeed, we have wondered whether he first sold the next round of retailers on the new strategy and, then, used their agreements to convince his family—Corning's top management—that the new strategy was a winner. The strategy was quickly extended across the nation. Here, bias was used as skilled bowlers use their knowledge of the bias of a particular ball, and even the lanes they are playing, to guide the ball to its target.

A Scientifically Designed Experiment at Anheuser-Busch

Now, let us turn to a more scientific experiment that played an important role in making Anheuser-Bush the world's leading brewer. Its success can be attributed, in part, to the fact that Busch became a learning organization in the 1950s, many years before this concept became fashionable. Busch appears to have maintained this character ever since, allowing the company to rewrite the rules of the brewing industry in its own favor.

Unlike Steuben's experiment, those at Busch were based on a controlled design demonstrating the flexibility of the experimental route to learning. In the 1950s, industry experts were betting on small regional brewers, such as Falstaff, which enjoyed a larger share of the St. Louis market than its neighbor, Anheuser-Bush, to be the long-term winners because, even as smaller brewers collapsed, Falstaff was able to buy capacity cheaply. Busch, on the other hand, was prevented by court order from buying a Tampa-based brewer in the late 1950s. Busch's response was to build capacity.

Busch built a new brewery and learned about the economics of scale, which set the stage for the modern U.S. brewing industry. Meanwhile Schlitz, the former number one market-share holder, and Busch's great rival for the next twenty years, learned nothing from Busch's experience and struggled in court for years over its own acquisition target: the Canadian brewery, Labatt.

Hence, while all of its competitors acquired, or at least tried to buy, capacity and market access, Busch learned to build bigger breweries and developed a competency that then led to future market success. Ultimately, the Busch breweries were of the 10-million-barrels-a-year class in contrast with the 1–1.5 million barrel plants of yesteryear, yielding production economies and a roughly 10:1 manufacturing cost advantage over Busch's regional competition. For years this advantage was hidden because Busch's heavy advertising and other expenses, which were used to buttress its distribution system and to fuel its growth, kept its reported profitability below that of the competition.

By levering its fulfillment capabilities between 1955 and 1975, Busch avoided strikes, preferring to settle labor disputes quickly with generous wages for its ABW Union employees. For the most part, these wage increases were passed on by the Union to the competition, where they hurt. The more labor-intensive small brewers suffered up to ten times as severely as Busch for any wage increase. All the while, Bush was learning to market and preparing for the next round of competition by slowly building its marketing competencies.

Busch also conducted controlled experiments in the area of advertising, and ended up with an enhanced marketing competency in an industry where margins are thin and the productive use of resources is essential. From 1963 to 1975, Busch deliberately sought to identify a more efficient advertising strategy by systematically varying the weight and mix of advertising expenditures across a number of small markets. For the managers who participated in these experiments, what mattered was not success or failure but understanding the outcome of this experiment, and dealing with its implications by formulating an improved advertising strategy. By sticking to small, carefully selected but out-of-the-way markets to limit risk and satisfy the chairman, management realized the real sales impact of their advertising campaigns, and that the beer market had an unusual S-shaped response curve. At the rate most brewers advertised, there was a positive relationship between advertising and sales so their spending made economic sense. But, at spending levels that were considerably less than the average advertising-per-barrel rate, Busch found another lower-cost, positive response zone. By using this knowledge and taking advantage of the company's growing size and total budget, Busch was able to redeploy its substantial advertising investment. This strategic shift was accomplished out of the sight of its imitators, most notably the now defunct Schlitz. According to data published in 1975 by consultants to the company who designed the experiments, Busch's advertising was so efficient that it changed the industry.[3] With hindsight, we can now say that Busch's plant expansion program was "effectively funded" by the savings Busch enjoyed against industry-average advertising spending levels. Pretax savings compared to normal advertising levels were sufficient to allow Busch to pay for a new at-scale brewery approximately every two years.

That their experiments and learning paid off is only part of the Busch story. The success of Miller's "Lite" beer in the mid-1970s was recognized by Busch as a turning point, whereafter the industry would no longer be the same. Miller's acquisition by Phillip Morris, and Phillip Morris's investments in at-scale breweries and its development and promotion of Lite beer, changed the competitive landscape. Now Busch, Schlitz, and Miller had the production economies to burn out the residual regional competition in the industry at an even faster rate than Busch and Schlitz alone. This done, the large national brewers turned on each other in an attempt to sustain their 10 percent growth in an industry where the average growth was only 2 or 3 percent.

By about 1976, Busch's leadership was being challenged, and its strategy that was anchored in production cost advantages, fueled in part by advertising efficiency, was no longer adequate. As the last of the regional players folded, the capabilities that yielded this advantage became necessary for survival. Marketing competencies then emerged as the differentiating factor and the new source of competitive advantage. Advertising was the largest marketing cost, and due to its earlier experiments, Busch was the most informed and efficient advertiser.

Busch acted strategically and broke the bounds of the old box by moving into what would, theretofore, have been seen as the supersaturated region of the sales/advertising intensity curve, well beyond the bounds of its own published experiments and industry history. Busch knew what to do. Recognizing that there are many ways to measure advertising intensity, with total dollar sales and dollars per barrel being two of them, Busch increased its spending on each of these two measures to levels that comfortably protected it from Miller's incursions, while preserving a very substantial return on investment (ROI) on its own brewing assets. The result was that Busch won. Miller survives but barely, suffering on with small accounting profits only. Schlitz died.

Busch was strategically aware and canny to boot because it had begun to adopt the mantle of a knowing corporation. Knowledge was created through multiyear experiments, with outsiders acting as counsel to top management, asking awkward questions and testing management's business assumptions. Knowledge allowed it to recognize the potential payoff from strategic change. Then, over an extended period of time, they used their knowledge of the emergent world to rewrite the rules in its favor.

A Strategic Experiment Redefines the Rules: Australian Paper Manufacturers

Sometimes, the result of a strategic experiment is a more rapid restructuring of an entire industry. In the mid-1980s, Australian Paper Manufacturers (APM) was forced to close a brown paper bag plant when plastic bags took over their market.[4] Australian Paper Manufacturers decided to experiment and see whether they could make white copier paper in this plant and find a market for that product. Having determined that they could produce such paper and that there was an attractive market for it, they entered, choosing to sell their paper products direct to the highest volume buyers: large corporations. This radical approach to product distribution leapfrogged long-established wholesalers who believed they controlled market access. By experimenting, using excess manufacturing capacity and integrated information systems, APM changed the structure of the Australian paper market.

Australian Paper Manufacturers, like Anheuser-Busch, changed the rules of the game in their favor. They had the will to experiment and challenged the status quo by doing the "unthinkable." The company crossed long-established industry boundaries by shifting the competitive balance between APM and its main competitor (PCA) and its customers and suppliers, thereby transforming the industry's value chain.

Where Are Today's Experiments?

We seem to be in danger of losing the administrative or managerial art of the strategic experiment. There are few examples today of experiments similar to the ones that were conducted by Steuben, Busch, and APM. In those experiments, learning directly impacted the company's strategy in ways that significantly differentiated them from their competition. Nevertheless, if we look around, we can see some organizations conducting strategic experiments to create an informed basis for changing the course of their enterprise.

New E-Business Ventures May Be Treated as Strategic Experiments

Australian Paper Manufacturers' experience showed that experimental market entries can be designed to assess the size of the market and the costs (human, knowledge, physical, and financial) of winning in it. When a market is new, such as the e-commerce market, an experiment is likely to help identify the risks associated with increased diversification and market unfamiliarity. Faced with global competition, IT advances, and the emergence of e-commerce, many successful companies in different industries will soon have to pass through similar crises and test their own windows of opportunity. If they fail to transform themselves in the right ways and at the right time, many will fail. It is not an option to simply wait for the results of other companies' strategic experiments.

Consider the action of John B. McCoy, who formed an Internet-only bank called Wingspan when he was the CEO of Bank One Corporation in 1999. Wingspan was one of a few such ventures at the time that provide customers access to a full range of financial products and services entirely via the Internet. A customer could use Wingspan to purchase mortgages, mutual funds, or insurance from among thousands of "virtually linked" companies. At the outset, it was not clear to the bank exactly how Wingspan would become a commercial success. However, McCoy reasoned that it was important to be one of the first big players with this business model, and that the only reliable way to figure out the strategy of Wingspan was to launch it, then listen and learn. McCoy stated, "I believe this is a new way to do business, and you'd better get involved with it."[6]

Learning about the risks and benefits of entry is the purpose of this type of experiment. Like most senior executives of publicly traded companies, McCoy probably did not talk about this initiative as an experiment because shareholders would rather believe their CEOs know exactly what they are doing and what the outcomes will be. Instead, when *The Wall Street Journal* asked him about his Wingspan Internet-only banking venture, McCoy simply responded: "All of a sudden now, there are ways you can go and get customers, without having the full brick and mortar. I'm not about ready to sit here and let somebody else take my business."[7]

But in private, McCoy and other CEOs like him—who have a track record of leading their companies into uncharted waters—intend to learn in action. And the learning is largely of a strategic nature, even though a considerable investment needs to be made in setting up the operating systems for acquiring customers and fulfilling their needs. Wingspan had a twelve-month budget of $150 million and the tagline "If your bank could start over, this is what it would be."

Bank One's potential payoff from Wingspan was grounded answers to open questions about the viability of an Internet-only bank. Relevant questions at the time included:

- What type of Web site will work best for the new set of customers?
- What will the customers' experience be with the security of their financial transaction and how will this affect the prospects for an Internet-only bank?
- Which options for handling customers' cash flows (in and out of the bank) will be acceptable?
- Is an Internet-only business model viable or will a hybrid model be required?

Sadly, Bank One may never reap the full value of this experiment because early in 2000, with Bank One's stock price down, John McCoy resigned from the bank, and his successor put Wingspan on the block.

Alliances Can Be Opportunities for Strategic Experiment

By experimenting and testing its business theories, either alone or with allied companies, management can make opportunities. Experiments can be easily conducted in current markets, or in new closely related markets where available capabilities or competencies give you an edge and moderate your risks. Partners may be helpful when you venture further afield.

In recent years, the number of business alliances has exploded. These alliances and networked supply chains are often intended to tap into the asset bases, capabilities, and competencies of other organizations so that the initiating company is able to pursue business opportunities cheaper and faster than if it tried to do everything itself. The best of the start-up dot-com companies—many of which seem to have more partners or alliances than paying customers—are doing just that. Not knowing where the greatest commercial opportunities lay, they engage in many simultaneous experiments, only some of which will prove fruitful enough to shape their future business model. At the same time, many established companies have the opportunity to view major contracts or alliances as experiments. Nortel Networks, for example, began to experiment with the use of contract manufacturing several years ago, when they fully embraced the strategy of large-scale transfer of their manufacturing facilities to a partner with proven success in this area.

Operational Experiments Test New Functional Strategies

The Andersen Corporation is the market leader in the U.S. window business and the largest window manufacturer in the world. Around 1990, one of its goals was to reorganize its functionally organized plant around groups of similar products to simplify and shorten material flows within the plant and to move the company toward continuous flow manufacturing. Rather than proceeding with a grand design across the whole plant at once, Andersen developed its new organizing concept by experimenting with a manufacturing strategy in two work centers of one subplant, using one for fabrication and one for assembly, to prove the new strategy's feasibility and to learn from the results. Andersen hoped that this limited initiative would provide an understandable model of the type of change the whole company would have to make.

And that is how it turned out. In 1995 management reported the rollout of the "plants within a plant" concept across their 2.7-million-square-foot factory, subplant by subplant, which was facilitated by insights gained in that first experiment. They also noted an additional benefit of experimenting—the immediate availability of concept-experienced people from the experimental units to work in the organizational units that were experiencing change for the first time.[5]

Ensure that Experiments Foster Organizational Learning and New Strategies

The recognition of a common objective or purpose sets the stage for collective learning. Without a shared purpose, individuals have little reason to reflect on the lessons or insights that their organization gains from its collective experience. However, when leaders test their theories through experimentation, they accelerate the process of knowledge creation and build confidence in the directions being taken. Confidence, based on grounded knowledge rather than on abstract visions and pure faith, becomes the source of reliable strategy and a foundation of meaningful leadership.

To generalize from the examples we have discussed, there is a powerful dynamic process at work when using strategic experiments to learn from action. It is a process that is primed by questions, powered by carefully considered experiments, and anchored by deliberate reviews of every result. Its purpose is to create new knowledge about the corporation's markets, proposed strategies, and process changes, and, thereby, develop new competencies. Ideally, this becomes a continuous process that loops through the experiments, results, and reviews over time, again and again.

This approach is motivated by the realization that, although there is a surfeit of data in business, there is considerably less information and knowledge about emerging business opportunities and how to seize them. Acting from grounded knowledge is preferable to jumping precipitously into a new business strategy in the absence of critical knowledge and tested competencies. And simply waiting for uncertainty to disappear is not a viable option for those who want to be the leading enterprises of tomorrow.

Deliberate experiments, therefore, are one critical step in a broader attempt to use grounded inquiry as preparation for an uncertain future. The other step is strategic learning from these experiments to ensure that what is believed about a company's competitiveness and adaptability is anchored in reality. Experiments coupled with the right kind of reviews become a powerful way to test your theory of your business as things change and to provide fact-based justification for new business ventures. When companies learn from their experiments, they can commit to new strategies with the confidence that only knowledge can bring. With experiments yielding questions and knowledge, strategic change can be purposeful, confident, and deliberate.

Taking Your Strategic EKG

Success in dynamic new markets can come from your having 1 percent more knowledge than your key competitors, and acting promptly on it. The way to do this is to follow up on your action-based experiment by explicitly identifying your knowledge gained. We call this process of identifying the lessons learned taking your strategic EKG (Experimental Knowledge Gained). Just as a medical EKG provides vital information about the functioning of your heart, your company's strategic EKG is a review process that uncovers the knowledge you need to ensure continued corporate vitality. Because knowledge is at the heart of your company, deliberately monitoring its development is akin to taking your own pulse.

With their own follow-up EKG, experiments can reveal the possibilities for new businesses and radically new ways of pursuing current objectives. First, as the examples illustrate, they give us data that describe the opportunities we think we can see with facts. Second, even when experiments do not work out as planned, management can learn something about the way to proceed by changing those strategic elements that it now thinks will work. Because a strategy grounded in experimentation and learning is based on insights gained from results that no one else has, it can become the basis for achieving new and distinctive competitive advantages.

For all these reasons, anyone participating in a strategic experiment must understand from the outset that learning is the objective, rather than whether the experiment has an overtly successful outcome. They need to appreciate the value that can be derived from engaging in a process of experimentation over a period of time, and looping through cycles of experiments, results, and deliberate EKG reviews. Acting from a base of newly developed knowledge does not eliminate uncertainty and risk; however, it is preferable to jumping precipitously to a new business model in the absence of critical competencies. Simply waiting for uncertainties to disappear is a recipe for disaster.

A successful EKG depends on having clear learning objectives for the experiment from the outset. Hence, a key component of the strategic EKG is to structure and analyze the results of the experiment, which creates information and reveals the actual answers to the questions that motivated the overall experimental effort. Then, seek new questions, which might lead to more sharply honed knowledge and even a new business model. You are already familiar with performance reviews that compare expected results with actual results. A strategic EKG must be more clinical than those reviews and include specific attention to the testing of assumptions about the business environment and the efficacy of the experimental strategy you used to deal with it.

In large experiments set up to test a new business model, you might use many of the concepts already covered in this book, for example, assessing the action alignment (AA) that you actually achieved to ensure that you truly understand the cause of your results. Similarly, you might thoroughly assess the degree and the nature of the strategic stretch you attempted, and ascertain the exact quality you created between your new customers' needs and your organizational capabilities and competencies.

Without formal commitments to EKGs, most organizations are unable to isolate exactly what has been learned and what should be learned from the blur of ongoing experience. To sustain the EKG effort, leaders at every level must be able to smoothly shift their thinking from the detailed results learned in the experiment to more general conclusions, future strategic implications, and next action steps. They must also allocate adequate time for all participants in this learning cycle to engage in needed analysis and deep reflection. That is where the EKG pays off—it ensures that failures are not buried but, rather, are made productive and earn their way.

Illustrating the EKG Process

To capture the full benefit of any experiment, the EKG must be tailored to that experiment; no general specification will work. However, to help you see how to do so, consider Microsoft's investment in Tandy in 1999. Consider it as a strategic experiment. When Microsoft announced its alliance with Tandy, it cemented the deal with a $100 million investment in Tandy's on-line store, radio shack.com. Microsoft stated that it planned to set up boutiques in RadioShack shops to sell its MSN Internet-access services and electronic products, including digital telephones, hand-held computers, and Web-TV. On the surface, this looked like a simple market extension through a new channel. However, it is possible that Microsoft was actually trying to build a new marketing competency by using this alliance as the vehicle.

If you consider the Microsoft-Tandy deal to be a Microsoft experiment, you will see why Microsoft is a formidable competitor. One hundred million dollars is not a large amount of money for a company that has a market cap in the hundreds of billions. And, although a large numbers of households in the United States did not own a computer in the year 2000, almost every U.S. home had a television. Finding a way to become the software and service provider to these noncomputer households would multiply Microsoft's value yet again. If Microsoft then sold Web access and software to the world market—a market that is currently categorized as either poor, less educated, or conservative—it could reach a market that is potentially big enough to multiply Microsoft's value several more times. So let us imagine that the Tandy investment was a self-funding experiment to develop Microsoft's know-how about consumers who either do not have computers or who are uncomfortable in today's retail computer stores.

Tandy could provide Microsoft with access to many of these people. The big question is, Can Microsoft learn what will appeal to these customers and what has stopped them from buying computers and Web service so far? If it can, Microsoft might be able to create new product or service offerings at prices these customers can afford, which are supported by promotions designed to assuage their concerns. Knowing how to create this knowledge is a marketing competence because its objective is identifying opportunities for sales growth.

How might Microsoft take its own EKG and review this particular experiment to expand its competency base? Use the following questions to get started, along with the possible follow-up steps that depend on the answers to the questions. The process can serve as a model for questions you might use for an EKG of an experiment in your company. Note that an EKG of this type would examine what actually happened and the results recorded, attempt to identify facts and causes, and the lessons learned and competencies gained.

> *Did we get access to the new customers we expected?*
> No. Was it a problem of customer awareness?
> No. Look for gaps in the order acquisition process.
> Yes. Recheck our theory of the business. Did we miss something important?
> *If yes, is there evidence of customer satisfaction?*
> Yes. Does our original estimate of market potential still look reasonable?

No. Reassess the business strategy.

If yes, does our original estimate of profitability still look reasonable? (document the real cost behavior)

Yes. Expand the experiment or initiate a new one if there are uncertainties. If there are no uncertainties, evaluate the merits of a full launch. Assess our risks, competencies, and capabilities, and the market's readiness for our new service or product.

No. Consider cost reduction possibilities and reassess the theory of the business that got us started.

If no, do we have the marketing and operations competencies to win in this market? Has our partner the requisite process capabilities and the competencies to warrant continuing the relationship?

Yes. Isolate delivery gaps in order fulfillment or postsales services (use the AA review from Chapter 2). Then ask: Can we create a more powerful set of business processes because of what we and our business partners have learned? Can we make a sharper division of what we will do and what they will do in our strategic partnership with Tandy?

If no, then have we failed to achieve (or even identify) a needed organizational competency?

Yes. Commit to a more targeted experiment to develop that competency or test contract or acquisition options to deliver that competency to this business venture.

Note that this experiment was about more than market sensing, which is a normal function of the marketing department. It was about experimenting with a new strategy for building Microsoft's business with a subset of its currently unserved customers. Coupled with a strategic EKG, the Tandy investment or experiment would teach Microsoft how to do more, or, in other words, to build new competencies to help it grow its business.

Conclusion

Although we may long for business visions founded on real foresight, such foresight is impossible to achieve. In our unpredictable social and economic world, the only reasonable basis for business visions and strategy is relevant insight based on grounded knowledge and a belief that we can make a difference. Grounded knowledge is learned in action, rarely from casual observation.

Intentional experiments are an essential part of the strategic arsenal of the knowing corporation. The successful use of experiments includes the deliberate testing of hunches about market opportunity, strategies, and the competencies needed to reposition a corporation for the emerging future. Managing experimental initiatives and harnessing them to the corporate purpose is always a challenge. But you can meet this challenge when you explore strategic questions with experiments, and then review their results in an EKG. Then, as you make follow-up decisions about developing new competencies and seeking better strategies, you will help your company become a more adaptive organization that is primed for success over the long haul. The quest for new competencies, or know-how, is critical because it is a quest for long-lived distinctiveness. It is a quest that demands insight and the deliberate effort to learn how to do something new.

Ideally, managers at different levels in the organization will come to understand this new knowledge discovery process and experiment within their own areas of authority. Many more will participate in larger-scope experiments by managing some elements of the action and collecting and interpreting the results. All these experiments should test key elements of a new strategy, and become an early step in creating new business opportunities by realistically gauging the risks. Members of such learning teams need to appreciate the power of failure as a foundation for productive learning.

Finally, at the highest levels, experiments also give CEOs some of the administrative flexibility that they need to do their jobs effectively. Only the CEO can commit the whole organization. Hence, deciding what can be risked, how long experiments should continue, and what pace of change the organization and its markets can withstand are all important judgment calls. To avoid the obvious dangers of turning the company in new directions too often, the CEO must deliberately control the pace of change and manage the rate at which he or she—*the big wheel*—turns. If it turns too fast, confusion will follow. If it turns too slow, opportunity will be lost.

Notes

1. Ikujiro Nonaka and Hirotaka Takeuchi, *The Knowledge Creating Company*, Oxford University Press, 1995.
2. Russell L. Ackoff, *Creating the Corporate Future*, John Wiley & Sons, New York, NY, 1981.
3. Russell L. Ackoff and James R. Emshoff, "Advertising Research at Anheuser-Busch, Inc. (1963–1968)," *Sloan Management Review*, Spring 1975, pp. 1–15; and "Advertising Research at Anheuser-Busch, Inc. (1968–1974)," *Sloan Management Review*, Winter 1975, pp. 1–15.
4. David Upton and Joshua Margolis, "Australian Paper Manufacturers," Harvard Business School, 1990, case #9-691-041.
5. Andrew Marine and Patrick Riley, "Creating a Culture of Change," *Hospital Materiel Management Quarterly*, Vol. 16, No. 4, May 1995, p. 30.
6. Rick Brooks, "Bank One's Strategy as Competition Grows: New, Online Institution," *The Wall Street Journal*, August 25, 1999, p. A1.
7. Ibid.

7
Using the Performance Measurement System

How often have you thought about your company's performance measurement (PM) system, or how well it impacts your work? When using the term performance measurement in this chapter, we are referring to the measures of organizational performance that are routinely aggregated and widely communicated, not to the localized indicators of an individual's performance that are traditionally used for personnel appraisal.

Few people think about aggregate performance measures until they have to. For example, when they are caught between a rock and a hard place because things have changed, they sometimes make an objective that they need to achieve unattainable. Usually, people tolerate what is already in place, or what they have been given, because they learn early in their careers that performance measures are not negotiable. This is unfortunate because when the environment changes and your strategy needs to change, you have to change your PM system to get anything accomplished.

In recognition of this need, some top management teams have instituted new company-wide measurement systems. A popular version of this system is the *Balanced*

Scorecard of Kaplan and Norton,[1] which has four principal measurement areas: financial, customers, internal processes, and learning. These measurement systems shift the focus of control from being exclusively on the bottom line to including the inputs that drive the bottom line.

If you work in an organization that already uses a measurement system, use the system that is in place to lift the performance of your own unit. If you do not, there is no need to wait for the top management team to adopt one. You can intervene with performance measurement enhancements that are useful to you and your operating unit. This chapter will show you how to do this.

A good place to begin is to think about the fit between PM and your company's culture. Doing this will help you to understand the general purpose and key structural elements of any PM. Consider which of the following phrases best describes your situation:

1. Measures do not have much value in our company.
2. Measures have a little value.
3. Measures are important.
4. Measures have considerable influence.
5. Measures dominate thinking.
6. Measures generate conflict and force trade-offs to be recognized and thoroughly considered.

The number of companies falling into the first two categories is usually small in comparison to the number of companies that fall into categories 3, 4, or 5. But, almost always, category 6 is thinly populated. If you can place your company in category 6, you are probably in a strategically aware organization and enjoy your work more than you would in companies where PM matters less. This last category describes knowing corporations.

Being in categories 3, 4, or 5 may be a sign that progress is being made toward category number 6. Or, it may be a dangerous dead end on the path to competitive advantage, depending on what is measured, who looks at these measures, and how they are used. For example, despite Wall Street's preoccupation with measures of profitability, these measures alone are insufficient to manage its progress forward in a fast-changing world—the bad news comes too late to avoid waste, and many opportunities to improve performance are lost.

The era of thinking that performance measurement is restricted to reports drawn up by accountants, the sales force, and plant managers is over. The knowing corporation broadens PM to include selecting, collecting, and structuring performance data on all key activities that ultimately drive the company's income. If a company does not broaden its measurement system to reflect all key dimensions of its strategy and make tough decisions based on what these measurements reveal, its new strategy is likely to be stillborn.

If you wish to succeed in the ways discussed in this book, it is quite likely that you will need to learn how to use the performance measurement system better than you currently do. First, you need to determine whether your current PM system is helping you to get the results that you are responsible for, and, if it is not, what you need to do to improve the situation. In particular, ask yourself these questions: Is PM a large part of your current problem? Are you ready to make the full investment required to make the PM system work, namely, using it yourself to direct behavior within your part of the company? And, can you align the PM system with the rest of the company's administrative systems?

Assess the Usefulness of Your Current Measurement System

Unfortunately, many companies produce reams of data that serve no useful purpose. In the 1960s, Marks & Spencer, the legendary British retailer, became famous for its eleven-ton bonfire of obsolete corporate forms. This symbolic act resulted from CEO Sir Marcus Seiff's attaching himself to a management report to assess who used it and why. He discovered that the report, and many others like it, served no useful purpose. His search strategy is worth trying if your reporting system is gummed up with useless information.

Ford took a different route and changed its PMS design when it tried to discover how its affiliate Mazda could function by using 10 percent of its administrative overhead. The Mazda executive team that Ford brought to the United States to audit its PMS reported that they were amazed at the amount, accuracy, and variety of information collected. They then asked, "Why do you collect it? What decisions depend upon it?" The ultimate result was long-needed change at Ford.

Later, at General Electric, Jack Welch followed up on Ford's experience. Welch discovered that at GE's appliance park in Louisville, Kentucky, the company was printing several cubic feet of computer printouts daily when, for the most part, the only decision was the number of white and colored appliances to be made. "De-bureaucratization" of the information system followed this discovery.

Perform a Quick Initial Check on PM Usefulness

How can you quickly assess the efficacy of your current PM system? First, take a corporate-level view and decide what has priority and why. Then, ask the following questions: How much have we invested in measuring performance in our company? How is the PM effort changing? Where is the effort greatest today? Is it on efficiency (for example, productivity) or effectiveness (doing the right thing)? Why?

Then, focus on the customer. Is performance measured in the eyes of the customer? How? How often? Do customer-specific performance measures impact compensation? How? Are performance measures signaling earning opportunities and problems early enough to be useful?

Then, move to your own operating level. How is the data contained in the PM system captured, verified, organized, cataloged, secured, made accessible, and distributed? Until it is distributed, information has only a waning potential value. The earlier, wider, and more deliberate the distribution of information, for example, the more likely it is that your organization is self-aligning. Find out who gets what data, what measures are used, and by whom? What conflicts are experienced and by whom? Where are the complaints? How are your own critical projects monitored through the performance measurement system? Is the system working with you and your business unit, or do you need to fight it?

Recognize the Structure of Your PM System

Regardless of their rank in the company hierarchy, managers need to recognize where change in their company's PM system may be warranted, why, and how to argue for changes that will help their companies to succeed. The key to doing so is to understand the structure of the current PM system. The following list outlines the major structural elements of a typical performance measurement system and what they do:

- ▲ Linking objectives and metrics to customer need focuses effort
- ▲ Widening the scorecard honors constraints, such as the need for profit and environmental compliance
- ▲ Monitoring organizational competencies ensures the company's future
- ▲ Timing and tilting the measures and stretching the

targets speed up or slow down strategy execution, adds pressure, and moves risk levels up or down

Assess Whether Your PM System Helps to Focus Action

In spite of all the management reports issued every day in every company, few managers intuitively appreciate the systemic impact of missed targets. Consider the order fulfillment process that is 98 percent on time, delivering shipments that are 95 percent filled, and 91 percent error-free. It is likely that the individual managers responsible for portions of the order fulfillment process are aware that their overall efforts leave 15 percent of the company's customers with some reason for dissatisfaction (1 − 0.98 × 0.95 × 0.91 = 0.15). That is no way to build a business! But, until the PM system is structured to present the full operational picture the way the customer sees it, managers may not appreciate that that their own unit's results are contributing to a growing overall problem. In these circumstances, operating systems need improvement. That is why the knowing corporation always seeks to learn more about its own impacts in its markets and how to better align its individual and collective actions with its strategy.

Increase Focus in Your PM System

A knowing corporation establishes its business strategy and then designs its PM system to fit it. Its objectives focus the action. Therefore, if you sense that action in your corporate domain is becoming unfocused, review your aggregate results against your contribution, profitability, and growth objectives, such as earning per share (eps) and eps growth. Use the raw template of Figure 7-1 to review how the objectives of each (horizontal) business process and

Figure 7-1. Functional and process objectives.

FUNCTIONS

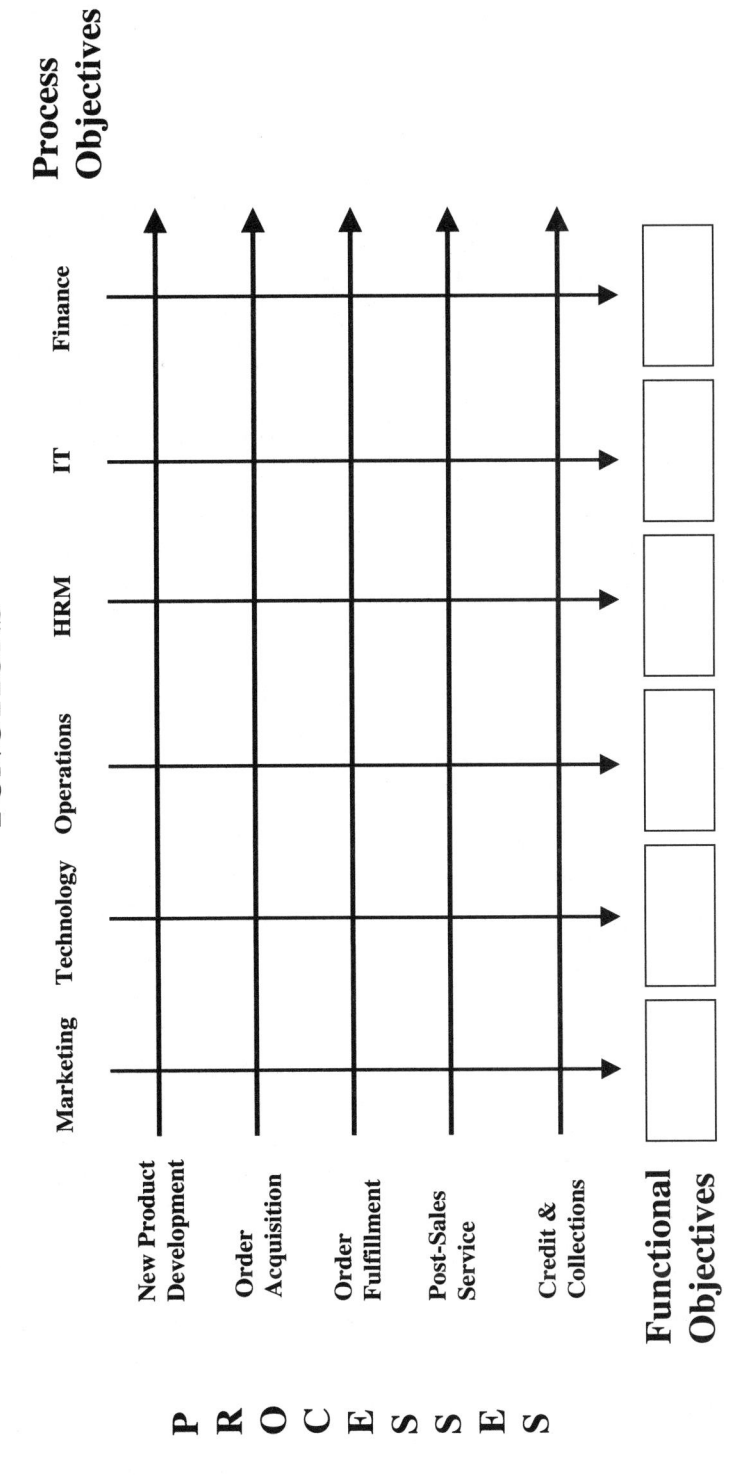

	Marketing	Technology	Operations	HRM	IT	Finance	Process Objectives
P R O C E S S E S							
New Product Development							☐
Order Acquisition							☐
Order Fulfillment							☐
Post-Sales Service							☐
Credit & Collections							☐
Functional Objectives	☐	☐	☐	☐	☐	☐	

(vertical) function are specified and how they contribute to profitability and growth.

The result of this initial round of work might produce a chart that looks like Figure 7-2, which was prepared for a PC assembler. Note that the core functions and processes that differentiate the company from its competition have been highlighted—here the core process (order fulfillment) and the core function (operations) have prominence. Carefully review the definition of these core objectives since they are central in the PC maker's business model. Getting them right pulls the rest of the system into alignment. If they are out of line, the focus you are striving for may be dissipated.

Now consider whether your customers' expectations have been fully satisfied. Typically, the first time around most of the objectives will be worded too generally to make a precise determination line item by item. But, the real issue is whether the action you are responsible for is precisely focused on your company's specific customers. However, until your objectives are focused that way, they are not concrete enough to drive behavior in the direction that you intend.

Therefore, if you are not satisfying your customers completely and your objectives are vague, consider sharpening their focus. For example, you might adjust the descriptions of your business's process objectives, creating a new chart like Figure 7-3. Note the increased customer-centering in Figure 7-3, as compared with Figure 7-2, and also recognize the increased longer-term character of the functional objectives listed in the last row of this revised chart.

If the objectives are on target but action is still less focused than it should be, another way to increase focus is to "operationalize" your objectives using more sharply crafted measures. Figure 7-4 lists a set of measures for the process objectives of Figure 7-3 to illustrate some possibili-

Figure 7-2. PC assembler's functional and process objectives.

Process \ Function	Technology	Enterprise-Wide Operations		Marketing	HR	Finance	*Process Objective*
			Supply Chain				
Order Acquisition							Get new and maintain old customers, converting first-time to repeat purchasers.
Order Fulfillment	**X**	**X**	**X**	**Core**	**Process**		**Give the customers what they require.**
Post-Sales Support							Maintain customer relationships and be responsive to customer needs and inquiries.
New Product Development/New Business Alliances							Be the first to market with new technology through alliances and linkages.
Function Objective	Create customer intimacy through interaction, information gathering, storage, and analysis.	Supply chain must be integrated throughout the enterprise. Produce high-quality product at the highest speed and lowest cost that matches customer specs.		Establish image consistent with consumer and business needs.	Create a workforce that is technically superior, effective at communicating, and consumer-oriented.	Maintain strong inventory and cash flow control system.	

Figure 7-3. A modern PC manufacturer/assembler: functional and process objectives.

Function \ Process	Marketing	Technology	*Operations*	HR	Finance	*Process Objectives*
New Product Development						Introduce a series of reliable easy-to-use products and services at costs below the competition, and at a rate faster than the competition can.
Order Acquisition						Consult customers about their needs and translate them into customer-specific orders with minimum number of steps
Order Fulfillment						*Deliver functional, reliable products and services on time with life-cycle costs that satisfy the customers or make them successful*
Post-Sales Service						Respond with certainty to customer problems and questions with minimum number of electronic steps
Functional Objectives	Define and open new markets for the company to sustain growth rate	Hold product design at SOA and maintain minimum number of electronic steps to customers and suppliers and reduce capital requirements	*Create integrated capital-efficient supply chain delivering reliable SOA product at competitively advantaged cost*	Create technically competent workforce with superior customer-relations skills	Arrange committed funding for business growth ahead of need at minimum cost	

ties. Note that every objective here has several tentative measures, each being a plausible performance driver for that objective.

Are the measures you use, or need to use, tightening your strategic focus on your customers to the dismay of your competitors? Again, given your results, are you satisfied with these measures or could there be better alternatives? What problems of interpretation and behavior do

Figure 7-4. Measures for customer-centered business process performance.

Introduce a series of reliable, easy-to-use products and services at costs below the competition, and at a rate faster than the competition can.

- Number of new products
- Sales per new product
- Rate of introduction versus competition
- Timeliness of market launch
- Reliability of product

Consult customers about their needs and translate them into customer-specific orders, with a minimum number of steps.

- Number of customer steps required to complete order
- Number and average size of orders
- Returns, complaints and compliments, and referrals
- Credit required

Deliver functional, reliable products and services on time, with life-cycle costs that satisfy the customers or make them successful.

- Backlog
- Timeliness of delivery
- Acuity of delivered product with scheduled order
- Condition of product as delivered

Respond to customer problems and questions with a minimum number of steps.

- Number of steps needed to resolve problem or address query
- Time required per query and variance of time required
- Feedback to the other business processes

---

they bring, and why? Discuss alternative measures, weighing their likely advantages and disadvantages, one against another.

When possible, shorten your list of measures. Fewer measures intensifies focus. Therefore, argue to eliminate measures that shift behavior out of line with your core business strategy. For example, the PC company's management did not accept "number of new products" as a measure. Unbridled proliferation of new products would complicate their operations, increase costs, and confuse customers. What they wanted, instead, was a limited number of core product platforms that could be customized late in the production cycle to meet a suitable variety of customer requirements. They wanted platforms that had competitive longevity—a very different design challenge for the product development group—and argued for them.

Note that by intensifying the focus of your operating unit's action you are clarifying the company's strategy for all the people reporting to you. In this way, your efforts to sharpen the PM system adds value by improving the way the organization is informed about the focus of its strategy and by helping you—and those you report to or work with—to recognize impediments to its success. Sharper focus in the PM system makes it clear to everyone in the organization exactly how you intend to serve your customers and to reach for profitability and growth.

The last line item in Figure 7-4—*feedback to the other business processes*—further demonstrates the dynamic effects of the PM structure. This ambiguous measure is simply not good enough to define what is required. Feedback is the basis of learning. The *number of messages* is insufficient because most companies want discrimination and impact, not just volume. Adding *number or contributions of changes following feedback* would help, although the changes made would be outside the direct control of the post-sales service personnel. Adding *requests for counsel* from the other business processes and functions might be another step in the right direction. As you sharpen this metric to fit your context and then monitor its progress, you will be better positioned to know what you are really trying to achieve and, later, the extent to which you have succeeded. To manage it, you must measure it.

In general, the PM structure should encompass a set of measures for each objective. Then, if the results achieved are not what was intended, you will be able to ask questions such as the following to help you make the case for change:

- Are there better ways to monitor progress success against this objective?
- Are some ways more informing? Which are likely to give us the earliest *heads up* that we are on track? Which is the most accurate measure? Which are most timely? What will pull us into alignment fastest?
- What are the drivers (key success factors) that managers will use to make their goals for these revised measures? Are they likely to have any unexpected and unintended consequences for us with respect to a critical stakeholder?

Widen the Scorecard

The steps discussed earlier will help you to monitor your company's performance against customer expectations within each operating cycle. Now we will discuss other measures of success and ways to satisfy the many constraints that are a real part of any business, for example, meeting capital market expectations and complying with the law wherever we operate. One of the ways in which corporations deal with these constraints is to include them as structural elements of their PM systems.

Companies must, of course, pay special attention to profitability. Performance with respect to customers, capabilities, and competencies is not sufficient to satisfy all of the company's stakeholders—*capital* has to earn its return for the company to survive. A failure to achieve operating profit on time is a strong signal that the strategy is incomplete.

Because profitability and economic value are already familiar concepts to you and your business, we need not dwell on them here other than as a reminder that unless a company can offer the promise of profitability it is impossible to capitalize on it, except impulsively for a short while. Leading companies make it a practice to set profit and growth targets that exceed their industry norms. They also include in their PM system measures that ensure that they are operating within the law in all countries where they do business. Measures of economic value and legal compliance, however, are lagging indicators of performance.

Modern PM, however, is intended to facilitate management interventions well ahead of the next annual, or even quarterly, financial report. To achieve this, the system's view of the company—for example, as represented by the AA model and the 3Cs—is necessary: Competencies yield capabilities, and capabilities yield customer satisfaction, which in turn is the basis for competitive advantage and, thus, profitability.

A PM system, widened in this manner, helps managers drive profitability by tracking their organization's capability and competency developments. When learning results in improved competency and capability, you will see positive impacts on customer satisfaction and sales, and, ultimately, on competitive advantage and profitability. Thus, you selectively widen the number of measures as a mechanism to drive performance, satisfy customers, and earn profits.

PM must also comprehensively address the company's relationships with all of its remaining stakeholders. Stakeholders are those who may exert significant influence on the company's affairs, both in normal and extraordinary circumstances. You want to monitor transactions and interactions with them to retain the inputs and cooperation that are necessary to keep the company in business. Accordingly, we recommend an even wider net than Kaplan and Norton's four areas for measurement—financial, customers, internal processes, and learning—so that management can consider the needs of stakeholders whose concerns are different before they concentrate on the bottom line. For example, in the oil industry, a prudent management team would monitor drilling, the operations of wells and terminals, transportation, and waste disposal performance against legal constraints and community interests, and even perhaps public opinion. And for multinational corporations, where success depends on the interaction of a variety of government policies and corporate strategy, it is always important to monitor performance with respect to all such existing policies.

Your company's PM system should keep track of every key stakeholder's short- and long-term performance expectations for your company. If stakeholder complaints and infractions are time-consuming distractions that deter you from pursuing your operating mission, your organization probably does not give those areas adequate attention in its day-to-day work. Adding explicit performance measures to these areas may make a big difference. By measuring the forces shaping every key stakeholder's shifting evaluations of your performance, your management team will be able to join the decision loop earlier than after receiving delayed signals from the bottom line. Seek leading indicators and monitor them to facilitate action rather than reaction—it is usually more expensive to catch the horse that is out of the gate than the one still inside the boundary fences!

Measuring Capabilities to Ensure Focus on the Customer

By eliminating bottlenecks and learning to manage their plants more efficiently, chemical engineers are accustomed to achieving annual increases of 10 percent in actual capacity compared with rated capacity. Companies in all industries can achieve key capability improvements by similarly tracking their own long-term process results. The possibilities for improved performance in all business processes have been enhanced because cross-functional management becomes the normal practice instead of the exception. How can the PM system support such efforts?

Returning to our PC example, the right-hand column of Figure 7-5 lists process capability objectives. Of the four business processes shown, the one that is usually most familiar for calibrating capability improvements is order fulfillment. Many manufacturing companies, when faced

Figure 7-5. A modern PC manufacturer/assembler: process capability objectives.

Function \ Process	Marketing	Technology	*Operations*	HR	Finance	*Process Capabilities Objectives*
New Product Development						time to market, product failures, warranty costs, product/process advances, ramp-up costs
Order Acquisition						number of calls required, consultative contacts, cross–selling rate
Order Fulfillment						*capacity, response rate, setup time, lead time, rework cost, cost improvement, incomplete shipments; on-time delivery, warranty costs*
Post-Sales Service						number of calls required, complaint/compliment ratio, conversion of problems into opportunities

with global competition, began to drive manufacturing performance. Establishing process capability metrics for the other three business processes may not be as familiar, and you may need several iterations to develop a list that fits your circumstances. Note that process capabilities can easily be defined in measurable terms. Furthermore, with the advent of integrated IT transaction systems, data on many of these capability performance measures are already being collected for timely monitoring and analysis.

Monitor Competencies to Protect Your Future

Organizational competencies are considerably different resources than business process capabilities. Despite what you have read here, you will probably sense this viscerally when you first try to measure them. While capability measures, such as capacity, setup time, lead time, response time, cost improvement, and on-time delivery, are precise and familiar dimensions of the order fulfillment process, organizational competencies—and the expertise that they embody—are not measurable in this way.

Complicating the matter further, the notion of organizational competency is almost meaningless when it is abstracted from effective action. This means that competencies are especially difficult to measure in familiar ways. And, since there is a tendency for managers to do what is easiest at the expense of what is more difficult, we recommend vigilance. Be alert to the danger of customer satisfaction and capabilities receiving too much attention relative to the company's competency development.

Deliberate action is called for to resist this shortcoming. To get started, classify the competencies you are applying by type, such as technology, marketing, or operating, similar to what has been done in Figure 7-6. Where you can, rank each of these competencies in terms of its competitive importance to your current business model. Qualitatively compare your functional competencies and inadequacies with those enjoyed by your suppliers, channel partners, customers, and competitors, and where the long-run competitive edge is likely to be. Although it is best to do this across your entire company, if that is not feasible, then at least do it for the operations within your own responsibility.

Figure 7-6. Monitoring competency development.

PC Business					
Function / Process	Marketing	Technology	*Operations*	HR	Finance
New Product Development					
Order Acquisition					
Order Fulfillment					
Post-Sales Service					
Functional Competency Objectives	Develop market knowledge, ability to use marketing mix in established markets, ability to assess new markets quickly and accurately	Master product, process, and information technologies and adapt company so that it is pushing, or is at, SOA in its core technologies	*Redefine what a state-of-the-art integrated capital-efficient supply chain is to ensure competitively advantaged capabilities*	Anticipate needs for new competencies within workforce and find ways to accelerate internal cultural adaptation to external realities	Anticipate and arrange committed funding for business growth ahead of need at minimum cost

One promising approach is to ask your suppliers, business partners, channels, and customers to judge your competencies, and the rate with which you are improving them with respect to the competition and their own needs. These two different points of view can be quite informative. Consider how long it has been since a supplier or customer asked your company for advice. How many of these calls do you receive every year? Is the trend moving up? How many organizations have asked to visit some parts of your organization to learn how to improve their own? All of these questions point to ways to monitor and measure competencies, and then to manage their development.

Look again at the descriptions of the functional competency objectives of our PC assembler in the last row of Figure 7-6. For example, it states the marketing competency objectives of this PC assembler as: *develop market knowledge, ability to use marketing mix in established markets, ability to assess new markets quickly and accurately.* Such phrases may appear quite fuzzy at first, but you can progress rapidly once you consider exactly how they might apply your company. Remember that you are trying to accomplish two things: (1) to identify the competencies that you will need to develop to implement your strategy successfully, and (2) to decide how to measure competencies over time and to determine whether they are developing fast enough to meet your future business requirements. By helping your company to establish this piece of the PM system in rough form at the start, you will avoid many disappointing surprises later.

Although GE had not been among the first companies to embrace e-commerce, it placed e-commerce initiatives near the top of its corporate priorities in 1999 for all business units. Consider, for example, how Jack Welch and his successor might monitor GE's e-commerce competencies. Internet purchases and sales would be lagged business results from such organizational competence. But what would be the leading indicators of growing competency in this new arena? Competency will grow as the company executes projects of e-commerce offerings throughout this multidivision corporation. Therefore, recruiting specialists will lead the organization's competency, and this will signal how much of the full array of competencies can be built within GE, versus bought through contracts or external partnerships. Then, requests for project funding can follow, and indicate some progress.

The competencies for GE's e-commerce strategy will be generated through the execution of a portfolio of projects aimed at e-business. Comparisons of one project against another will help management and the project teams will gauge their growing competency. Partnership interest in this new way of doing business will follow. Then, sales, growth or purchases, and the significantly reduced capital that is required by buyers and sellers alike—especially relative to the competition—will point to competency development.

As this GE example shows, competencies are similar to projects. They develop through milestones or along time-linked trajectories. With some artfulness, we can find ways to monitor our progress and to honestly assess in real time where our organizational competencies provide competitive advantage and where they do not.

Set Targets: Stretch, Time, and Tilt

When your business is focused, your constraints honored, and you have a sure eye on the long-term interests of the company, you are in a position to shoot straight. It is no longer "Ready! Fire! Aim!" but "Ready! Aim! Aim! . . . Fire!" Targeting allows you to choose the amount of energy to exert for any objective as you execute your strategy.

When you set performance targets, you are taking a definitive step toward achieving your objectives. Defining objectives, setting performance targets, and measuring achievements over time are essential steps in converting strategy from raw concept to detailed plan, and, ultimately, to results. Holding people accountable for specified results is another.

Investing in PM is one of the costs of building an aligned, adaptive organization. But performance measurement can not stand alone because it is at the center of several allied administrative systems, one of which is the compensation system. Therefore, you should review your targets for every objective and measure to realize the full benefit of your PM investment. Is the stretch large enough to be simultaneously attainable but motivating? Are people stretching to achieve them and, thereby, earning their just rewards? Are you holding yourself and them accountable, and doing everything you can to make genuine success possible?

As an example of how to set targets and insist on accountability, consider how you can manage process performance improvement through managed learning. A powerful guide to setting specific performance targets for most business process performance dimensions is to calculate the half-life of performance improvements. The half-life is the time it takes to achieve a 50 percent reduction in defects, such as errors, rework, unnecessary reports, unscheduled downtime, employee turnover, setup time, or warranty costs, that impact or measure performance or any other performance improvement. This is a phenomenon that is familiar to quality control experts who attempt to improve delivered quality to 4-sigma, then 5-sigma, and then 6-sigma levels. It is also quite familiar to most general managers, who are well aware that effort can move an organization down the experience curve where costs decline with accumulated output.

Analog Devices Corporation pioneered the monitoring of operational progress against competitively determined half-life targets for performance improvements. The approach used was to identify defects and their principal causes, and then to find ways to eliminate them. Similar measurement-based improvement processes, such as

6-sigma quality programs, are used at Toyota, Motorola, and GE, just to name a few. In the integrated circuit business, similar performance-improvement phenomena are captured by formulas of technological possibility—represented by Moore's Law and Rock's Law—that project targets for improving price/performance ratios for integrated circuits. The lesson from all of these performance-improvement programs is to establish aggressive but feasible targets, and, then, work to make them happen.

When you review your performance targets and ask what impact they are having, recognize that performance improvement is a social process. Assess how well your process performance targets are tied to accountability and then rewarded. Rewards should be crafted to encourage behavior consistent with the company's objectives. Unfortunately, experience suggests that this is difficult advice to follow. The following questions will help keep the project on track:

- Do your performance targets allow progress to be monitored by frontline workers, supervisors, and managers?
- Is there a strategic rationale for every performance-improvement target?
- How well do your performance targets match the critical role of a particular business process in your strategy, regardless of whether it is owned or contracted? How do your unit's performance targets differ from those of your company's other businesses across all business processes?
- Can you verify that the effort to boost performance on each target will have a positive competitive impact?
- Have you identified who is accountable for the desired result? Accountability is crucial in the performance management process because it triggers action.

Finally, there is a test that will reveal how well you know your company's PM system: Do you know enough to tilt, or shape, the behavior of people reporting to you, and thus realize the immediate priorities that directly affect your ability to achieve your goals? Tilting is the dynamic element of performance management. It helps you to transcend the present and to seize opportunities as they emerge. It means taking the company in one direction or another, depending on the information flowing from your PM system. The goal here is to respond to your scorecard by dynamically seizing opportunities where you can by shifting targets—shortening deadlines, stretching further, reaching higher—while avoiding the opportunism that could threaten your organization's integrity and long-run interests.

In a knowing corporation, managers set new priorities in light of changing political, economic, social, and technological forces that shift the company's profit potential, and its stakeholders' relative power. Tilting the operating scorecard is a key mechanism for responding to these changing priorities.

Some of the most powerful tilting strategies include setting goal-based incentives, shifting some deadlines forward, lifting target levels up or down, and establishing detailed time-based trajectories of accomplishments. Some companies achieve additional tilt through a combination of metrics, culture, rewards, and recognition, without ever attempting a full scorecard approach. For example, 3M earned decades of exceptional results by managing investment decisions to achieve a set of fixed, well-publicized, corporate-wide financial and new product development targets, while building a culture of innovation throughout the company. Ironically, these performance results were extraordinary because all managers believed in the culture of innovation, not because they had a PM system that isolated the building of particular customer-relationships, process-centered capabilities, or functional competencies.

A leading company in the white goods industry has moved even further along in the use of performance metrics. This company's traditional strength in manufacturing has been driven by rigorous cost and quality metrics. But, despite its distinguished reputation along these lines, its lack of an innovation record in this mature industry may be due to the fact that, until recently, it had not measured the performance of its product creation process. By the year 2000, this company was emphasizing product innovation and the building of brand equity as cross-functional drivers of success in their global business, but, once again, these objectives were not explicitly reflected in specific metrics. Perhaps, in this case, the lack of measurement was due to this company's traditional functional orientation, which distracts it from being fully customer-centered, and the fact that it was late in confronting the problems that had arisen from neglecting its own PM system.

Uncover Other Performance Measurement Problems

It is worth knowing what some of the most typical PM problems are because they are, in fact, alerts that change may be warranted. Among the most common are complaints that employees cannot access the information they need, unknown *mis*-measurement that leads to mismanagement, and the type of PM mimicry that leads to convergent strategies within an industry and the loss of a company's distinctive competitive position.

Needed Information Is Not Available

Senior managers repeatedly tell us that they cannot get the timely information that they need. This is usually a sign that their PM system is being run according to the fiscal calendar rather than the business calendar, and that it is dominated by financial reporting requirements, consistent with externally accepted standards of accuracy. Poor information and managers who feel that they are "kept in the dark" are related signs that the PM design is flawed. Performance measurement must go beyond the formal accounting system and, instead, be fully supported by the company's management information system (MIS) and appropriate technology. If this is not the case in your company, you should argue for change.

We frequently hear the organizational maxim, "Don't expect what you don't inspect." Front-line workers directly inspect the results of their labor to boost performance. But managerial inspection is more indirect and must rely on performance measurement systems. Over and over again, executives tell us that one problem at the top is determining where to allocate scarce time and where to get the information they need. Ironically, however, when questioned, very few can prove that they have selected the measures that are represented in the reports that cross their desks. The simple reason for managers to invest in the design of their PM systems is to make it useful for their own decision making.

Some systems fail because they are too heavily burdened by managers who believe, "If you can't measure it, you can't manage it." This often results in measuring everything that can be measured in conventional ways and ignoring the rest. A related problem is effort that is wasted in a fruitless attempt to measure everything according to the same standards of accuracy, regardless of the costs and benefits of the data collection effort.

Misinformation Leads to Mismanagement

Despite widespread interest in activity-based cost management, misunderstood overhead allocations continue to be one of the most insidious problems in performance measurement. Do you know how your operating data is shaped by overhead allocations?

Some years ago, the managers of a long-established manufacturer of kettles, ovens, and other equipment for the food-processing and food-servicing industries added a new product line to their traditional offerings. One difference between the old and new product lines was that the new line was considerably less labor intensive than the old custom-ordered product line. This might not have mattered too much except that this company was also very oriented to the bottom line, with a corporate management that maintained a hands-off approach, unless the bottom line delivered unhappy news.

With little interest in the forward control of their subsidiaries, it was no surprise that top corporate management left one significant element of the traditional accounting system in place—the way overhead was allocated in this subsidiary company. Old and new products carried overhead that was allocated in proportion to direct labor. Hence, it was not long before the business's management team began to find its old labor-intensive product line underbid on once-reliable contract prices while its new product line began to receive inquiries from several very large prospective customers attracted by its competitively low prices.

On the surface, things looked well. Change is, after all, a constant even for old-line manufacturers. Indeed, a casual observer might have complemented management on their prescience in pioneering the new line in time to make up for the loss of business now being suffered by the old. But casual observers would have been misled.

The company's overall profitability was falling, and, because of the information delivered by their PM system, management believed that high labor costs in its traditional lines was the problem. To help rectify the situation, and despite a backlog of orders, the company took a strike of several weeks at its old plant, choosing to alienate their loyal customers in the pursuit of lower costs. What a casual observer and, more significantly, management, could not see was that they were reacting to false information. They had changed strategy but not their performance measurement system, and the information it produced was misleading them.

The real situation was that their efforts to accelerate the growth of their new business had increased corporate overhead considerably. But in accordance with their long established practices, the accounting-dominated PM system allocated overhead proportional to direct labor hours. Therefore, most of this new expense was allocated to the old labor-intensive lines. And, because the old line was overburdened with overhead allocations, the new line was underloaded.

One result was that management tried to lift prices in its old line and lost business. These losses compounded the company's unit overhead cost problem and cut management's confidence in the future of its prototyping and consulting business—which had been the golden goose that had sustained the company for almost fifty years, because it had few competitors and none with its exact fulfillment capabilities.

Worse, the company's apparently low costs in their new higher-volume, lower-labor-content new business led to another problem—overconfidence and the naive belief that they could live off the new line alone if they landed one large contract. They also became convinced that they would be able to compete with several much larger suppliers because of their "low" unit costs.

Therefore, the old, unchanged performance measurement system, and their own failure to understand the accounting models it was built upon, led them to ill-advisedly turn from their old business to the new. Their decisions were ill-founded. They began with a false premise. Their information was unreliable.

Other Causes and Cures

When everyone competes in the same way and achieves the same levels of performance on some dimension of performance—for example, low-cost or 6-sigma quality—that once conferred advantage, these dimensions no longer provide an edge, but instead have become necessary for survival. Casual adoption of benchmarks and competitors' standards of performance as your own goals can lead to the trap that many, including Harvard professor Michael Porter, have called *convergence*. Convergence occurs when managers, seeking to achieve the same goals, drift into using similar strategies, often being drawn to the optimization of the same single business process rather than their own deliberately chosen strategy. With convergent strategies and "shared" accomplishments, the capabilities deployed become insufficient for advantage.

The cure here is that PM specification is a choice of the company's targeted performance levels. When targeting performance, management should be guided, but not dominated, by the company's past or by its competitors' performance. Whether the issue is profitability, setup time, or competency development, for example, you need to be careful not to simply mimic the performance of other organizations by adopting comparable business processes. Also, make the effort not to blindly pursue noncomparable corporate benchmark experiences and results. Only adopt those that you have determined to be relevant to your own company's customers and other stakeholders.

When there are measurement problems like these, they are almost inevitably a consequence of management's abdication of authority over their performance measurement system. Instead of promoting focus; helping the company to honor its realistic constraints; helping it to prepare for the longer-term future; and sensibly balancing pressure and risk with the capabilities, competencies, and experience of the company and its managers, the PM becomes a source of confusion. Rather than facilitating and supporting the delegation of responsibility to others, and testing them with checks and controls, it creates cynicism and destroys morale.

Too often PM design is left to those in accounting, or some other function, who have biases and perspectives that are incompatible with managing the company as a system. Sometimes the PM system is simply accepted "as is," allowing probably long-dead accountants to continue to hold sway over the company's future. Management has to have real-time and relevant information to change things while there is still time to choose a better way. And, this is clearly impossible if senior operating managers abdicate responsibility for PM to corporate history, and the dead. By abdicating, they miss an opportunity to shape the future of their organizations and to correctly focus its efforts.

Conclusion

When you *mis*-measure, you mismanage. If you measure what you do not use, you waste time and slow your own decision processes. Therefore, the design of the PM system must deal with customer satisfaction and the bottom line. It must reflect every organization's need to honor the constraints imposed by its many stakeholders, including the government. And it needs to deal with specific competencies and capabilities too, since they will determine your strategy's potential. Then, it is up to you to use it and tilt the competitive balance in your favor.

Using the PM system efficiently demands effort. Whenever there are substantial changes in the business environment or a change of strategy, there often needs to be a change in the PM system. And, from time to time, the data the PM produces must be tested and, occasionally, restructured since new conceptual structures are needed to turn ordinary data into fresh powerful information. All of the approaches presented in this book that deal with ongoing operations and strategy—the AA model, the 3C test, and the stretch test—embody the assumption that your management team will mine your own performance data for new questions and new answers in its search for critical knowledge about your business. In addition, historic comparisons—comparable and competitive comparisons over time and across products, markets, and processes—and timely benchmarks can be used to give the output of the PM system greater value. Anticipation and fast reactions are the products of informed judgment, founded in knowledge and competence, based on assessments of your company's and your competitors' results.

However, there is an art to using the performance measurement system. Whether recent results point to future success and failure depends on many factors. What they mean in the short run may have little consequence for the long. Managers at all levels continuously need to sort out the facts and weigh them to make their own diagnosis of the current situation—to divine the meaning of today's results for tomorrow. Success favors managers who anticipate change and use their company's PM system to frequently ask, "Why?" When we evaluate strategies, what we see will depend on when we look, and what we see will depend on where we sit.

Whenever you are trying to get a new strategy or part of a PM design team in place, seek leading measures that will allow you to test the match between your current circumstances and your strategy while you still have time to choose. Focus on understanding critical dimensions of external and internal change. Try to identify and remedy any internal or external biases in your present measurement system. Remember that:

- The risks you choose, and the measurement systems you use, will either shackle you to your past or foster adaptation.
- Most successful companies drift to a position of reactive strategic retentiveness over time, and risk declining fortunes, while working hard to survive repeated crises—including those they make for themselves.
- High-growth companies favor actively changing strategic postures but have their measurement systems tilted toward longer-term, externally focused measures.

Ultimately, management must react to the company's successes and failures, no matter their cause, in real time. For all practical purposes this means taking action before the lag that applies to most legally required financial reports. When supported by effective IT and used by executives who have the will to manage, well-designed PM systems facilitate rapid adjustments, like the missile guidance system's "Aim! Aim! Aim! Aim!"

Executives in knowing corporations use their PM systems to promote continuous learning, strategic acuity, and higher levels of operating performance. Value accrues through multiple, rapid evaluation cycles—formally, if needed, but otherwise informally—by the managers whose hands are on the switch. A well-designed PM system allows management to coach and strategize, and to empower others to make decisions that improve performance.

Note

1. Robert S. Kaplan and David P. Norton, *The Balanced Scorecard* (Cambridge, Mass.: Harvard Business School Press, 1996), p. 9.

8
Getting Everyone Involved: A Knowing Culture

No matter how well your company was positioned for success five years ago, you are probably embracing quite different ideas today. And, if you are to be successful in the future, not all of these strategic ideas will stand the test of time. You must develop new opportunities and new strategies to survive. The ongoing restructuring of our global economy, however, is exposing even established companies extraordinary opportunities, if they have a culture that favors adaptation and the capabilities to seize them.

Create Knowledge for Corporate Survival

Knowledge—the only sustainable source of competitive advantage—must be created and applied as a corporate way of life if you are to survive. Therefore, the real winners will be companies that make knowledge management a living reality throughout their organizations. A few, such as Motorola and GE, have achieved extraordinary results at operating levels with 6-sigma quality programs, which build a culture of best practices by sharing and applying operating knowledge throughout the corporation. The bigger challenge, however, is at the strategic level, where the initial requirement is creating knowledge rather than sharing it.

There are plenty of stories of radical product breakthroughs achieved in informal skunkworks by teams of inspired individuals who were drawn from the middle ranks of large companies. Much less common are tales of organizational transformations that were triggered by strategic discontinuities but driven from the middle. Top-down transformations are certainly the norm in the business press no matter where they originated, because the capital market likes to know that the "jockey" is in control of the horse. The reason is simply that formal power resides at the top. But in the knowing corporation, formal power is less a catalyst for change than is informal power driven by knowledge and, as we shall describe next, a healthy view for organizational politics.

IBM's dramatic shift to a strategy based on e-business was rooted in ideas and initiatives that percolated up from the energy and accomplishment of a few dedicated self-appointed champions in the middle ranks of the organization, as strategy consultant Gary Hamel has explained.[1] The result was that, by the end of the 1990s, IBM had grown an Internet-consulting business of major proportions. Key elements of this transformation included the following factors:

- In 1994, IBM computer programmer David Grossman learned about the emerging Internet technology and sensed its potential revolutionary impact.
- Grossman took the initiative to demonstrate early Internet capabilities to some executives at IBM headquarters and captured the enthusiasm of John Patrick, a middle-level staffer with a marketing

background who was responsible for strategy formulation. Grossman's knowledge and enthusiasm convinced Patrick to become an informal sponsor of additional work on this theme.
- Grossman and Patrick became an informal team. Patrick brokered resources to implement demonstration Internet applications that Grossman developed. Patrick also broadly conveyed the message that the Internet needed to be an IBM-wide business opportunity, rather than the mandate of a single business unit.
- CEO Lou Gerstner was intrigued by their project, and became an early symbolic ally and significant supporter.
- Patrick and Grossman took advantage of the 1996 Summer Olympics as an opportunity to demonstrate Internet capabilities, drawing favorable external attention that would, in turn, build credibility with internal executives at IBM.

The rest, as they say, is history.

This story illustrates the process of transforming a mature top-down company that needs shaking up. But in a knowing corporation, there will be many success stories like this one, and the need for fewer shake-ups. That is because the organizational culture will favor, rather than resist, knowledge-based action of this type, such as the project initiated by IBM's informal coalitions. In short, more midlevel players across the corporation, like Grossman and Patrick at IBM, will take the initiative to build the right competencies for their company.

Building competencies is necessary because competencies underlie capabilities, and capabilities yield satisfaction and competitive advantage. Advantage and profitability is, therefore, the product of conscious organizational effort, not spontaneous insight. No distinctive competency means no advantage, and no profit! We have seen how the knowing corporation establishes a solid ground for operational alignment, strategy development, risk management, and strategic experiments as precursors of advantage, but how does one develop an organization capable of doing so continuously?

One executive pointed out how difficult it is to recognize the need for transformational change when business-as-usual is so demanding:

> We live on crisis [sic] around here; they're normal. Every day our competitors try to twist our tails and we shift 'em, grab theirs, and squeeze. That type of crisis is everyday fare and the way we cut our teeth, earn our stripes . . . that sort of thing. We all know how to handle these. What I'm talking about is the nagging worry that something's wrong, and getting worse, but you can't quite catch it, yet you feel it's going to force you to fundamentally change the way you do business.

Another executive, the CEO of a large defense contractor, described one of the costs of failing to discriminate between these everyday crises and the business-shaking crises that demand new ways of thinking and managing knowledge as follows:

> We have a tendency to act rashly without discriminating as to the nature of a crisis rather than being afflicted by analysis paralysis. We treat everyday crises and transformational crises identically, and so give too little effort to the transformational. It's hard to deal with the big opportunities and disasters ahead when you've just successfully avoided the consequences of yesterday's disaster.

Clearly, it is best if your organization's learning is initiated before the need for new knowledge becomes crucial. The emphasis that we have been placing on experiments and stretch strategies promotes learning to learn, exploring change options, and creating new opportunities. And, as Thomas Edison is said to have once advised Robert Merck: "Your experiments may not work out as planned, but they are the only way to make your own opportunities." But we should remember that it is easy for the window of opportunity to close before the company is ready to respond.

One reason why the window closes is competition. As industry leaders experiment and learn how to break away from the pack, they precipitate transformational crises for their competitors, making the need urgent for those who follow them. Another reason opportunity passes is caution. Every company has the problem of recognizing impending crises, and the need for transformational change, in a timely manner. But companies whose managers cautiously try to ensure that they are correct before committing to action will almost certainly be too late to market. Such caution is the antithesis of learning in action and the adaptability that it fosters.

Consider how adaptive strategic learning impacts companies. If you have experienced a successful organizational transformation, you have probably noticed that decisions that critically impacted your organization's ability to recognize the need for change were made at two levels. First, an operating manager like yourself gets a hunch, has a nagging concern that does not quit, or sees that something is up and decides to do something about it, beginning by raising questions that are worth investigating. Then, at some point, either the senior management team or the CEO, whose own behavior and decisions shape the company's ability to learn, must commit the organization to a new course of action. If the company has a "learning culture," such change may soon be under way. Otherwise, the manager who initially raised the questions is likely to become frustrated, and either become ineffective or have to spend substantial amounts of time working surreptitiously around the organization.

That is what happened at Teradyne in late 1996, when its chairman and CEO, Alex d'Arbeloff, become concerned about the long-run implications of his company's commitment to UNIX and to developing its own software. As a board member of a small start-up, he had observed how quickly a company could move to market by using Windows NT as a platform, and investing far more selectively than Teradyne did in software development. The small company had parsimoniously invested only in domains where it had distinct competencies, and purchased other needed software at low cost from the thousands of programmers working with the Windows NT platform.

Although he was Teradyne's chairman and CEO, d'Arbeloff resorted to setting up an off-site skunkworks to develop a new generation of automatic testers for integrated circuits. But that had a cost. Later, after the new technology had been proven, he found reintegrating it with his corporation's ongoing operation to be complex and difficult, because he could not convince his divisional managers to pick up the project as their own. The case for change was clear to him, the product worked, but he had insufficient support to bring it to market quickly—the case, or the way it was presented, was unconvincing.

Create "See, Screen, Search, Sign, Sell" Chains

Teradyne's experience suggests that an organization can develop an expanding base of grounded knowledge, recognize the need for transformation, stay on track with reality, and be ready to change in a timely manner only when a good case and support are built simultaneously. Then, this approach to fundamental change can be made standard practice at the organization. The objective is to make adaptability part of the organization's culture through a process of corporate-knowledge creation and sharing that we call the knowledge ignition process, as outlined in Figure 8-1.

The process has five steps: (1) recognition, (2) formal screening, (3) informal searching, (4) signing, and (5) selling. It offers you the time to think politically about bringing any issue to senior management's attention, so that you get time and attention to bring the case for change forward.

Acknowledging the politics of change is central to success. Since D'Arbeloff was unable to engage his divisional managers in the development of his new testing equipment, his company paid the price with slower movement from prototype to full production than might otherwise have been the case. The rough handoff that occurred between the skunkworks group and ongoing operations was the price of a political failure—in this case, dysfunctional office politics rather than self-serving behavior. Strategic change, like Teradyne's, almost always requires face-to-

Figure 8-1. The knowledge ignition process.

1. Seeing early indications of fundamental change in the external business environment
2. Screening for personal risk, likely support and opposition, and defining the strategic questions to be researched
3. Searching for answers with experiments of several types
4. Signing up peers and colleagues, and getting their commitment to further research the questions and interpret the results—even if their commitments are transitory
5. "Selling" the findings about markets, strategies, and needed competencies to senior management for action, whatever the issues and questions discovered, and with strategies evaluated

face negotiations, political savvy, and substantial effort from its champions to be sustainable. That is what d'Arbeloff provided for Teradyne's new generation of automatic testers for integrated circuits. But the task for champions like d'Arbeloff will be easier if you can institutionalize the process described by Figure 8-1 within your organization.

Figure 8-2 presents this same management process as a sequence of steps moving from the initial recognition of the question to action along a chain described by *seeing, screening, searching* and *signing up,* and, finally, *selling.* At this point, if the signed-up team is successful in passing the cause to a higher level, outsiders can be called in to help validate observations, assess implications, and add the tests of their experience, new information, and questions to the debate as needed.

Once this knowledge ignition process has taken root, it will lighten the burden placed on any single manager who believes that he has seen cause for change, by establishing a legitimate forum for defining and sharing knowledge and debating the issue. In this way, the knowledge ignition process helps to transform the organization's culture into a more adaptive form—the knowing corporation.

The first step in this practical learning-in-action process occurs when an operating manager, in the course of his or her everyday ongoing responsibilities, realizes that something significant to the future success of the company seems to be changing in unexpected ways. Teradyne's d'Arbeloff was in this situation because of his external board experience. But, in fact, early recognition can be stimulated by a wide variety of sources, including formal environmental scanning. Most often, however, it stems from the ability of one person, in the right position and at the right time, to recognize the significance of a pattern that he or she has not seen before. To some extent, serendipity is in play. But the company's future does not have

Figure 8-2. Knowledge ignition: from recognition to action.

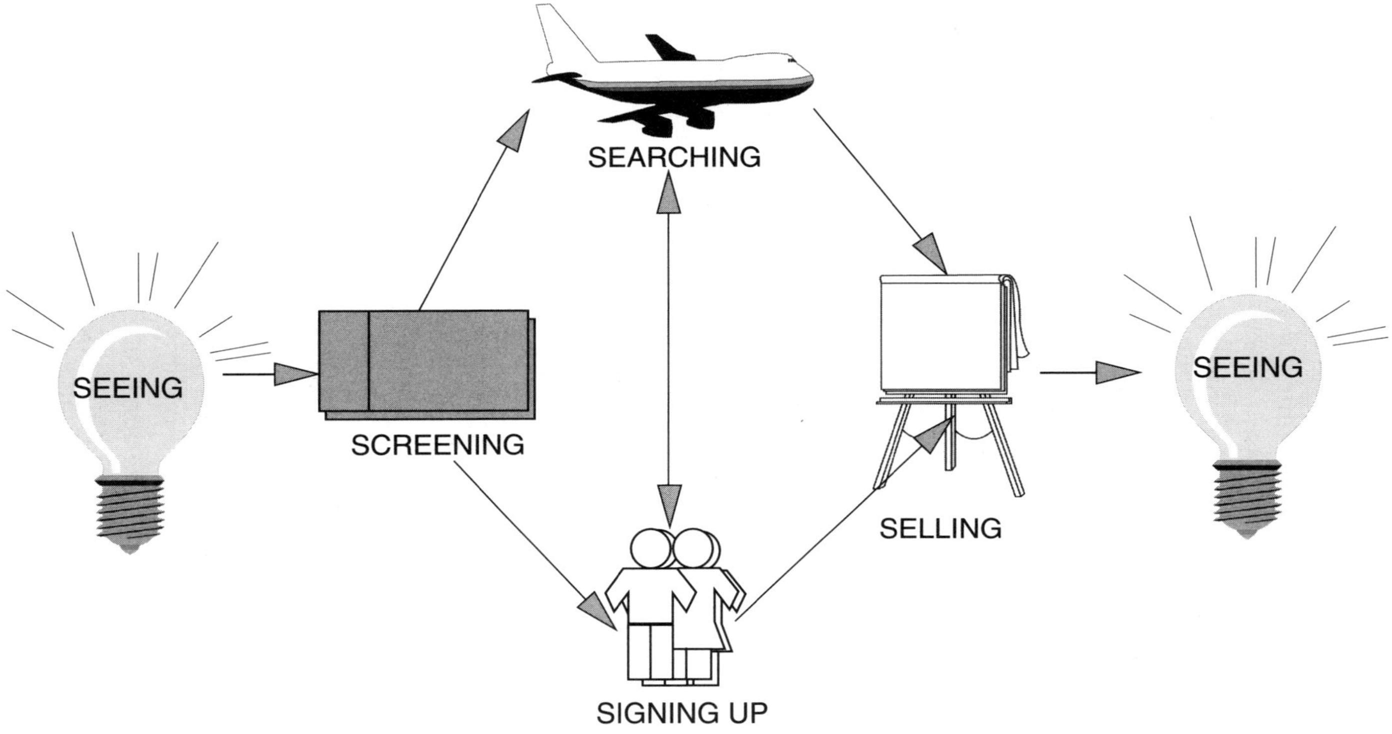

to be left entirely to luck if the remaining steps of the knowledge ignition process are in place.

The second step in the process is where organizational ignition begins—when this same individual decides whether or not to move the issue forward at the current time. Taken on as an individual responsibility, this step requires careful screening on two dimensions: to assess the level of personal risk associated with bringing the issue forward and, second, to carefully frame the strategic questions needed to precipitate action. Companies that have already institutionalized learning with strategic experiments, EKGs, and well-crafted performance measures will have considerably reduced the personal risks of raising such questions and putting the organization's knowledge to work. For others, screening includes assessing the politics of the organization with respect to the issues that are of concern to it. It is important to determine where the votes are, and why, and deal with that political structure as a real part of the situation.

The third step, conducted simultaneously with the fourth, is to build the case for transformational change by searching for answers to the original strategic questions and for evidence that appropriate change is feasible. D'Arbeloff's skunkworks fulfilled that role at Teradyne. The fourth is to sign up a coalition of key managers and staff members to advance the learning effort. That is the step that d'Arbeloff found difficult and time-consuming despite—or perhaps because of—his executive position. In part, this may have occurred because Teradyne had no formal process for dealing with D'Arbeloff's concerns.

In contrast, the knowledge ignition process is a practical and legitimizing form of EKG that institutionalizes a new forum for the champions of change to sign up supporters so that the organization can further investigate any perceived strategic opportunity or threat. Often, an informal mode of knowledge creation directed at nagging questions is possible. In any event, the supporting coalition, once formed, needs to establish a knowledge-based case to convince others that a commitment is needed. In the best political tradition, expression of the case may have to be customized to win one important vote at a time. Along the way, every coalition will experiment, learn, and possibly benchmark against other competitors, to create a critical mass of knowledge and, then, to reach out to others. Like most corporate coalitions, any initial coalition is likely to be short-lived and bound together more by concerted action than by unified long-term objectives.

Sometimes the search process is impeded by what Harvard professor Dorothy Leonard-Barton has called core rigidities.[2] Core capabilities can become core rigidities because they have both advantages and disadvantages for a company. The key idea is that accumulated knowledge is a powerful force, until the situation changes. Then, paradoxically, well-established capabilities may inhibit the development of new knowledge. It is a form of insularity or silo thinking that can suffocate initiative. Indeed, rigidities of this sort within his operating divisions blocked d'Arbeloff's efforts.

When explaining how these rigidities arise, Peter Drucker warned that the cognitive maps or theories of business that helped management to create the capabilities now in place have been so effective that there has been limited need for paradigm-breaking problem-solving. In such cases, you would expect to find, at best, only limited experimentation, and, even more debilitating, highly selective screening or filtering of external information. For organizations that are afflicted by a cultural inability to innovate with new tools and methods but blessed with substantial past success, it will be difficult to employ the approach suggested here. Ironically, these situations are where it is often the most needed. It is consistent with Andy Grove's observation that it is difficult to promote "strategic dissonance"—that is, thinking that runs counter to the strategy that has already been in force—in a successful operating organization. The fifth step, finally, occurs when the managers in the change coalition become convinced, and then committed, to selling their case to a broader coalition that will include more senior managers.

For the knowing corporation, Figure 8-2 is only a single cycle of what can be a longer, multiyear process of learning in action. Reducing the uncertainty surrounding any proposed change to the point where management is prepared to act unequivocally may take many individual learning cycles. But, no matter how many cycles are required, management must expand the company's knowledge base to the point where its options and the consequences of a wider commitment to a new strategy are clear. By this point, the CEO, and most members of the senior management team, will become committed to action.

Figure 8-3 illustrates a two-cycle learning process, a kind of chain reaction of building coalitions and cases, all triggered by the initial *seeing* step in the first cycle.

CEO Caveat

Despite the best efforts of the public relations industry to promote the image of a heroic CEO as the sole champion of change, this is usually not what happens upon closer examination. The multicycle process view of transformational change presented in Figure 8-3 emphasizes that insight and the learning that grounds it are not the exclusive province of top management. On the one hand, to be fair to the PR folks, their mission is to convince the capital market that someone smart and energetic is firmly in control of our corporations, so their position is understandable. But, to be realistic, the demands placed on CEOs in most large organizations rarely allow them the time to person-

Figure 8-3. Igniting a chain reaction.

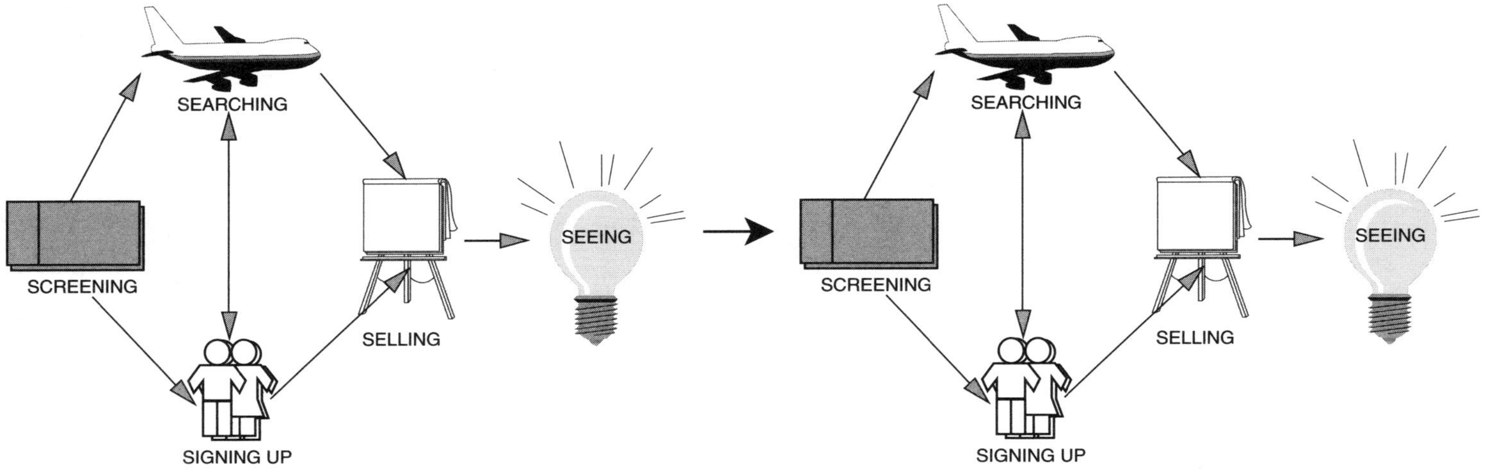

ally develop the case for change within their own organizations. The only exceptions are CEOs who are hired for the purpose of turning a company around, and, even then, their election is usually based on a powerful board coalition's diagnosis and prescription of the right medicine.

Additionally, in most cases, even if the CEO were able to jump-start the seeing process and quickly express his or her concerns about the company's future, there is always the substantial risk that the organization would overreact to those concerns, simply because the CEO *has spoken*. The risk is that senior managers, eager to please the CEO, do not make the effort to accurately judge the scope of the danger or opportunity. The tendency is to move to action too quickly—and, possibly, become too distracted to pursue other more pressing opportunities in the company's core businesses.

Intel's rise to prominence, and its ability to stay on top in a rapidly changing industry, is testimony that processes like Figure 8-3 work, even when powerful CEOs are in office. It is commonly known that CEO Andy Grove was a powerful force at Intel, and responsible for much of its success. For our purposes, it is interesting to observe that his success seems largely to be due to his reliance on a process like Figure 8-3. Grove listened to middle managers, allowed strategic market experiments, and committed the organization's full energy to new programs when the way ahead became clear. For Intel, the path became clear faster because they were experimenting, and because their middle managers were able to commit resources to successful programs without board approval.

Intel became an adaptive organization through its step-by-step collective awakening at the end of its DRAM memory business and its realization of the full potential of its microprocessors. Over several years, this process ultimately maximized the acuity of its emerging strategy. Our argument, however, is that waking the company up should not be either the province of luck or the responsibility of one lonely manager whose self-appointed role is to sound the first alarm. At Intel, in each cycle, a wider spectrum of managers provided information on what they believed and had observed, contributing to the knowledge creation process and, therefore, reducing the uncertainty surrounding a new strategy.

There is no getting away from the political character of large-scale change or from the fact that it takes time. The challenge is to act effectively and give the issue a fair hearing as early as possible. Then, it is a matter of using the company's knowledge resources to overcome bias and error, such as lazily but incorrectly confirming the ever-comfortable notion that "nothing significant has changed"—the classic "what I knowed that just wasn't so" error referred to in Chapter 5.

Accelerate the Action-Learning Process

Institutionalizing the knowledge ignition process is one more step that you can take to help your company become a knowing corporation. Figure 8-4 outlines some key elements in this conversion. Some of these elements may be familiar to you, but we present them here as an integrated approach to accelerating the conversion process. When all the leverage factors are used skillfully, learning will be second nature, and crises and opportunities alike will be recognized early, then evaluated and dealt with appropriately.

Support Managers Who See More and Learn Faster

The individuals who will help the company to see more and learn faster should be more than highly trained staffers, and be given wider authority than their staff activities

Figure 8-4. Elements of the action-learning process.

To see more and learn faster
Listen, face reality, and encourage debate.
Put the right people in key positions.
Do not mix transformational decisions with routine staff work.
Develop informal networks both within and outside of your organization.

To infect the organization with urgency of crisis
Do not confront individuals or assign blame.
Set the stage for discretion and experimentation.
Implement the scan, sign, search, and sell model.
Use consultants for external validation.

To move the organization to action
Resolve conflict in favor of change.
Replace those who block all change.
Allocate resources for experimentation and change.
Reorganize around successes and reward the leaders of change.

would normally encompass. Bean counters, critics, or cynics who have a narrow view may handle the routine responsibilities of their positions well, but if they lack good business sense and entrepreneurial skills, they will suffocate the future hopes of the company or your business unit. These people will be responsible for presenting both sides of the equation—the internal and external case for change versus the case for no change in the light of a wide set of criteria. They must carefully investigate and resolve mismatches and gaps in thinking. Because this role is so important, it is worth thinking about the qualities of persons selected to fill it.

As we have argued throughout this book, the greatest contribution that operating managers can make to accelerate the learning process in their organizations is to face reality squarely, encourage debate, and channel conflict in constructive directions. They must refuse to deal with anything but reality, even when it hurts—that is, the price of a learning organization and of a fast response capability. Any manager can assess his or her own performance with respect to all these issues by honestly answering one broad question: Am I receptive to divergent thinking? Listening is the key requirement, and this key but very personal ability will be reviewed in Chapter 9. In this chapter, we will deal with the types of people who make learning possible, practical, and, ultimately, profitable.

People need to agree on a course of action because consensus is the foundation for co-aligned action when executing strategy. However, in contrast, independent thinking and constructive conflict are usually necessary inputs to winning strategy formulation. Debate, therefore, is not a sign of disloyalty. The active or tacit suppression of debate, however, is a sign of insecurity at or near the top. Some senior staff, for example, aggressively filter information flowing to their CEOs to "protect" them, or, more likely, themselves.

To see more and to help the organization learn faster, management must carefully select and evaluate the performance of the people they have placed in key positions that provide access to critical transformational signals of either emerging problems or opportunities. They must also ensure that these people have time to develop a deep understanding of the issues and opportunities facing the company.

Although many people can sense an impending crisis, only a few are able to both see the need for change and initiate the learning process. Top management, therefore, needs to recognize the characteristics of managers who are likely to spark knowledge creation and share in an organizational context that may have internal political overtones. These managers need to demonstrate the ability to see what is acceptable inside the organization, evaluate it in light of what is expected outside, and maintain and develop a wide variety of useful informal networks both inside and outside the organization. In addition, they probably have already demonstrated technical or functional competence inside the company and the ability to fit with, contribute to, and use ongoing strategic knowledge created by others. Finally, they must have an unquestioned commitment to improving the organization's performance. These key participants are likely to be functional and process managers who have ongoing responsibilities in marketing, new product development, and capital budgeting, and are already influencing strategic decisions critical to meeting the company's product, process, and investment targets.

For the knowledge ignition process to take root, transformational decisions should not be mixed with ongoing budget and formalized strategic planning. Individuals who can get the right issues on the corporate floor for debate will normally have already demonstrated that they can maintain a wide set of relationships within their companies, because informal internal networks are needed to foster coalitions and constructive debate before, during, and after experimentation. They also need access to outside networks that expose them to ideas from beyond your corporate boundaries so that they can test some of their own ideas without risk. In particular, they need to venture beyond their own organization's boundaries to personally experience the currents of world change. This can be accomplished by visiting benchmark companies, which is often an important experience that modifies a person's definitions of good and inadequate performance and a stable business future.

When evaluating key personnel, also consider the depth and breadth of their business and in-company experience. Experience appears to add significantly to a manager's ability to see what others cannot, and, later, to express what he or she sees in terms that are persuasive to the organization. Personally lived experience is more quickly synthesized and integrated into intuition than any other type of learning. In particular, it is likely to support an accurate intuitive "mental model" of the organization that helps these people quickly sense political threats, organizational sensitivities, and resistance to change. Such awareness allows them to work effectively in both the formal and informal structures of their organizations.

Finally, these individuals need to be more loyal to the organization and its performance than to individuals or ideologies. They should have reputations as good listeners because this ability allows others to talk to them without the need to screen their thoughts or perceptions, as well as allowing them to see what others do not.

Infect the Organization with Urgency

A knowing corporation is skilled in creating a sense of appropriate urgency. After all, knowledge acquisition can appear to be a frivolous exercise if the whole management team feels that all is well. On the other hand, effective leaders realize that they cannot accelerate the learning process by simply confronting their organizations directly, thereby diverting attention to personalities and away from shared issues. So, when it is necessary, a more subtle infection of the organization with the urgency of crisis is called for.

The knowledge ignition process sets the stage for the use of discretion and experimentation, both formal and informal. The screen, sign, search, and sell activities described earlier serve this goal because they combine attention to the politics of change with shaping the case and defining its urgency. Promoting reinforcing sets or chains of such activities helps to ensure action and change better than any one executive speech.

When the new direction, despite the evidence at hand, seems to be a hard sell, a proven tactic is to seek external validation. Here is a key opportunity for the use of outside consultants. It's more effective to use them in this role than as a substitute for your own process of organizational learning.

Move the Organization to Action

Even in an era characterized by Internet time, patience is needed when moving the organization into a new strategic direction. By moving too soon, CEOs risk confusion in their organizations, wasted opportunities and resources in existing markets, and even their credibility within their organizations. Moving too late similarly risks failure.

In this context, the shortest path is not necessarily the direct path to learning and knowledge. Savvy managers try to act when change is needed, but only when the case for change is supportable in terms understood by those internal and external stakeholders with veto rights. Timing is everything, and good timing is founded in good judgment. It takes patience and persistence not to deliver the message until it is both presentable and defensible. Therefore, the impact of experimentation and review processes will sometimes be greater if formal top-level participation is delayed. Likewise, it is advisable to avoid premature formal evaluations of emerging ideas and strategies because ill-considered tests put the organization at great risk of being wrong.

Despite these warnings, accelerated learning requires managers to resolve conflict in favor of change whenever possible. This will often mean replacing those people who have a chronic need to block change. Management can also indicate their predisposition for change, even under ambiguous conditions, by allocating resources for experimentation. Once the case is clear, they must find resources to support the change that is needed. In the end, they need to reorganize around success, and reward those people who contributed to the success of the change effort. These steps ensure an organizational climate within which the knowing corporation can thrive.

Conclusion

World-class competitors solve their problems quickly. Typically, these companies are committed to increasing their competitive advantage. They strive to be Number 1, even if they are currently Number 2. They are combative and have the ability to turn on a dime once they recognize that an opportunity or problem exists. And yet, if you look closely, you will see that the best of them act with deliberate speed when it comes to large-scale business transformations. They can afford to do this because they start early and follow an approach similar to the one presented in this chapter.

One of the defining attributes of a knowing corporation is a culture that embraces the wisdom of testing, and then breaks traditional or long-standing business rules in the pursuit of advantage. Knowing that your organization is going to be at a strategic crossroad is a good start to creating a successful future. But knowledge alone is not enough to sustain your organization's success. You need to commit resources to change before change is needed.

Such corporations are able to create new competencies, capabilities, and customer relationships. However, their success is sustainable only when founded in continuous organizational learning, fueled by asking and answering questions about possible sources of diversification and new growth. Doing this means overcoming the normal tendency to think that success can be sustained only through incremental performance improvements.

In this chapter, we have provided an approach for overcoming the entropy associated with success—setting up and using the knowledge ignition process repeatedly until it becomes part of the organization's culture. The knowing corporation goes beyond the comfortable zone of periodic formal reviews into the less familiar but more potent zone of timely exploratory probing, informal strategic experimenting, and entrepreneurial coalition-building.

Ultimately, knowledge management is a social act that demands political skill to impact the whole organization. It is not limited to technical expertise, but also encompasses market sensitivity and managerial competence. Knowledge management is founded on learning from ongoing action and deliberate experiments. Only when commitment yields cultural change will the full power of a knowing corporation be sustained into the future.

How will your company face its most significant, and least acknowledged, sources of uncertainty? Are you able to create your own future strategic options—that is, new ventures in directions not predetermined by your history? Do you have the types of processes and people in place to break away from the pack at the right time? Do you attract and retain the best employees by having an engaging, exciting, and effective process of learning in action? When both uncertainty and the stakes are high, is your organization able to learn with *see, screen, search, sign, sell?*

Notes

1. Garry Hamel, "Waking Up IBM: How a Gang of Unlikely Rebels Transformed Big Blue," *Harvard Business Review*, July–August 2000, p. 137.
2. Dorothy Leonard-Barton, *Wellsprings of Knowledge* (Cambridge, Mass.: Harvard Business School Press, 1995), pp. 41–45.

9
Leading with Knowledge: A Personal Agenda

The members of a management team were asked to compare their roles in the company with the principal parts of an automobile. One replied that he was like the tires, working to ensure that the rubber meets the road. Another said that she was like the steering wheel, guiding the direction of movement. One member claimed to be like the headlights, illuminating the path ahead, while another saw himself as the power train, driving the organization to change. But when the CEO responded by saying, "I guess you could call me the hood ornament," there was an awkward moment as the other participating senior managers stared at their feet in silence.

In the knowledge economy, leaders in the corporation who are hood ornaments—and the companies they adorn—will face tough times. Instead, as we have explained throughout this book, there are specific approaches you can use to lead with knowledge. We will begin this final chapter with a short review of the leadership challenges of knowing corporations, and how to meet them. Even if you are not currently part of a knowing corporation or firmly situated in the executive suite of your corporation, you can still begin instilling its ideals and approaches within your unit. Then, to help you do this, we will examine the personal price you must pay for success in this pursuit. The best leaders are often most noticed after they are gone. And you will be too if you have listened and learned and built an adaptive organization with the ability to create new knowledge. You will not be a hood ornament.

Meeting the Challenges of the Knowing Corporation

You are now familiar with the following three fundamental challenges that you need to meet to make your organizational unit, or even your entire organization, more knowing:

▲ *Sharing knowledge* about every business process and its contributions to your business success. By applying the AA and 3C models, your people can be fully informed about your objectives and strategy, how they may directly impact its success from their levels, the advantage it can yield, and the impediments they have to overcome to achieve its potential. The knowledge that they share helps to make your operating system customer-centered and to work at its maximum potential. By using six generic business functions and five business processes interacting in the AA model with thirty alignment checks, the overall strategy and its various components can become clear to all. Where problems are identified, the audit process that you have learned ensures that they will be thoroughly evaluated and addressed, which strengthens alignment and, ultimately, customer satisfaction.

▲ *Stretching with knowledge* to new opportunities, enhancing and deploying existing capabilities and competencies to build advantage in new markets. When thinking is stale, the stretch test you have learned helps your people to broaden their perspectives by getting them up on the balcony, where they can develop a fresh corporate-level perspective. This test helps them to find new ways to frame issues that need to be addressed. It encourages them to test their ideas and to learn, through trial and error, more about the risks of any new strategy and how to extend the limits of organizational flexibility. Without knowledge, people venture carefully, if at all, and play it safe. Or they wing it, and risk avoidable disasters. By identifying and assessing the risks associated with your stretch initiatives, you can decide whether go or no-go is the right response, and, if it is go, how to manage those risks. Prudent leaders ask people to do what is possible. Responsible leaders position them to win.

▲ *Seeking and creating new organizational knowledge* and learning to apply it. To succeed, begin by experimenting in small ways to develop the confidence to do greater things, including the development of the organization's executive depth. You will combine your experiments, which can be testing grounds for future leaders, with EKG reviews to ensure strategic learning in action. To the extent you can, you ensure that there is always a resource reserve for these planned yet informal experiments in support of strategic change. Such resources support your people when they take experimental action, which—although not formally authorized—will further develop the case for change either in markets being pursued or operational improvements.

This book provides you with an agenda for pursuing these three related challenges. To help set the stage, you now have a model for building a culture that supports ongoing experimentation and knowledge-building. And you have a road map for developing a performance measurement system that allows you to tilt behavior to achieve your strategic objectives. Your PM system, coupled with specific performance targets, provides knowledge-based guidance on the extent to which your organization is accomplishing its objectives.

As you lead this stretch to the future, do not abandon the managers whom you wish to test by throwing them in the deep end to see if they can swim. Instead, manage their development. EKG reviews, for example, become forums where your company's key decision makers become familiar with each other's thinking, knowledge, and biases, and so it makes sense to include people below the senior ranks in the EKG process. Participation in the EKG not only helps managers to challenge their own thinking, and to avoid groupthink within the organization, it also allows them to gauge the vision, imagination, and courage of their management teams. For example, because only a small number of executives have the native ability to switch their thinking from analysis to synthesis and visioning, participation in EKG sessions can alert participating senior managers to gaps in their own executive capabilities and the need for development. Furthermore, by visiting benchmark companies, your people can personally experience the currents of change and be better positioned to modify their team's expectations about good performance and emerging trends in their business.

Despite the simplicity of the AA model, the tight but simple structure of 3C-stretch evaluation, and the discipline of an EKG review, some managers leap to action on a hunch and short-circuit the process. When any of these evaluation processes is short-circuited, however, actions tend to be equivalent to shots in the dark that may or may not hit an important target. The penalty for skipping the steps is often an unpleasant surprise that could have been avoided had a more knowledge-based approach been followed. If this has happened to you, or if you have to clean up after someone who has been caught, simply go back to the basics, review the situation, and do what is right with new knowledge to guide you.

Preparing Yourself to Lead with Knowledge

The decision of whether or not to convert an entire corporation into a knowing corporation is a top management decision. Maybe you have that authority, or maybe you do not. But even if your authority is currently curtailed to your business unit or function, or one business process, there is much that you can do using this book to make your unit more knowing, and therefore more successful. But there is a personal price to pay: You must prepare yourself to lead with knowledge.

Here is a four-step agenda for you to follow. First, you need to hold yourself accountable for the future of your enterprise business function, process, or unit. Consistent with this view, your thoughts, words, and deeds must be compatible with your vision and strategy, no matter where you sit in the organization. Sharing leadership, communicating, and testing your management are important, but you must also *walk the talk*. No doubt you already understand the implications of this requirement. Second, you probably need to practice listening more effectively. Third, you should expand your leadership style and become more flexible in selecting the approaches to use. Finally, you may need to change your attitude toward reorganizations. Because the last three steps are less obvious than the first, we will elaborate on each of them.

Learning to Listen and Listening to Learn

Active listening is a catalyst for change within any business or operating unit because it overcomes some of the distance created by authority and promotes questions. Leaders who practice active listening signal a genuinely open door and demonstrate care and respect for those doing the talking. In this way, listening is engaging, informing, and promotes learning. Such leadership requires both the ability to ask good questions and the discipline to be attentive and silent—unnatural behavior for many take-charge executives—to hear the questions that trouble others.

To appreciate the significance of listening, consider the basic structure of modern management. There is an inherent mismatch between authority and responsibility in all companies. Nurturing constructive behavior in the middle of complex organizations, where the responsibility to know often exceeds the authority to act, is a key objective for leaders who learn to listen and listen to learn.

Active listening at the top is a prerequisite for meaningful dialogue in the middle. Nothing will kill genuine dialogue faster than a senior manager who is unwilling to listen and, thereby, demonstrates little patience or respect for people or what they may want to say. The practical reason for listening, then, is because the authority concentrated at the top of organizations has limited potency. Knowledge and competency at the top are always less than what exists throughout the management team. In practice, then, the leader is dependent on his team to identify opportunities, likely strategies, and competitive reactions, and so it is only by listening that we too can be fully informed.

Listening also facilitates effective delegation. Effective delegation promotes flexible and more adaptive organizations, characterized by managers who have all learned to think for themselves when exercising their authority. A management team with these competencies stays "in formation," as IBM's legendary leader Thomas Watson liked to say, and develops deeper organizational competencies from these so-called formations. Even large organizations, with considerable but diffused resources, such as GE, can credibly say that they can behave like nimble, small companies with shared knowledge to rapidly shift their strategic direction.

Throughout this book, we have described how the prospects of any organization's survival are enhanced by sets of reflective questions asking why we do what we are doing, and whether it should continue. However, unless leaders listen, such questions are unlikely to be asked, and the company's initiatives will lack strategic content. Therefore, strategic change will be by fiat, executed through a rigid command structure—probably with ineffective results, given the uncertainties and competition that abound in the knowledge economy.

No manager can assume that the communications he or she receives are entirely frank. You need to ask questions to root out the truth, especially when things are going wrong slowly. (Remember the apocryphal tale of the frog calmly letting itself be cooked in slowly warming water, rather than sensing that it was time to jump out?) You need to listen to what is said and hear what is not. And you must not take for granted that the normal cross-functional communications within your organization are meaningful and robust. Instead, you must actively encourage and nurture openness if you want the real issues to be dealt with. And you will have to learn to listen, too. Andy Grove, when he was CEO of Intel, described his personal experience with listening this way:

> In the face of a strategic inflection point, voices sounding danger ahead will emerge. These voices

usually arise from the middle management ranks or from the sales organization: from people [who] know more because they spend more time outdoors where the storm clouds of creative destruction gather force and—unaffected by company beliefs, dogmas, and rhetoric—start blowing into their face. Some will flag their concerns to top management—and it's wise to pay heed. Others will just quietly adjust their own work to respond to the strategic change. Often these words and actions don't seem strategic at first glance: They seem peripheral. But it is wise to keep in mind that when spring comes, snow melts first at the periphery: That's where it is most exposed.[1]

Grove learned that listening opened the gates that were impeding the upward flow of information to the top executives at Intel. Listening enabled Intel to discover the causes of dissonance that Grove almost missed when the Japanese took over the DRAM market. It is because of experiences such as these that Grove recommends that all managers listen carefully so they can get the information they need to sort out whether the "times are a-changing"—forcing a critical decision at what he calls a strategic inflection point.

For centuries, people simply—and literally—put their ear to the ground to hear the rumblings of an approaching warrior band of soldiers or bandits. But what should today's business leaders listen for? And how can they do it?

Do what this book says. Listen for the knowledge you need to align your operations with your customers. Listen for the sounds of your organization stretching to be certain that you are testing your mettle and taking affordable risks. Listen, too, for the sounds of opportunity and knowledge needed, or being created, and the signs that you are developing your competencies and executive depth to ensure continuity over time. Knowing corporations recognize these to be the standard set of issues that shape your future. And, although one or another may require special priority at a particular time, none can be neglected for long.

Be More Flexible in Your Leadership Styles

Successful leaders use the full armory of change levers available to them and patiently extend their reach throughout their careers. An example of this leadership challenge is shown in Figure 9-1. You now know how to frame certain problems in terms of a troublesome function/process intersection on the AA model, as illustrated in the background of Figure 9-1, that identifies where you and your organization face a critical problem. Then the organization needs to develop a solution, and you may have to intervene with appropriate administrative changes to make it happen.

Experience tells us that the solution to any business problem involves selective changes to staff, skills, systems, structure, strategy, and, occasionally, shared corporate values. These, along with style, were the 7-Ss model widely used by McKinsey & Company.[2]

Strategy, as currently defined, is represented by the functional process network of the AA model at the top of Figure 9-1. Skills, staff, systems, structure, and shared values are listed on the horizontal axis of the front chart in the figure. Sometimes, change along only one of these dimensions is called for. Sometimes a few of these dimensions need simultaneous adjustment to allow you to realize the full potential of your strategy in the market.

However, the quality of the planned strategy execution and the effectiveness of any administrative change—and, therefore, the organization's success—will also depend on the style of intervention you personally make; for example, consulting, directing, coaching, or challenging. We

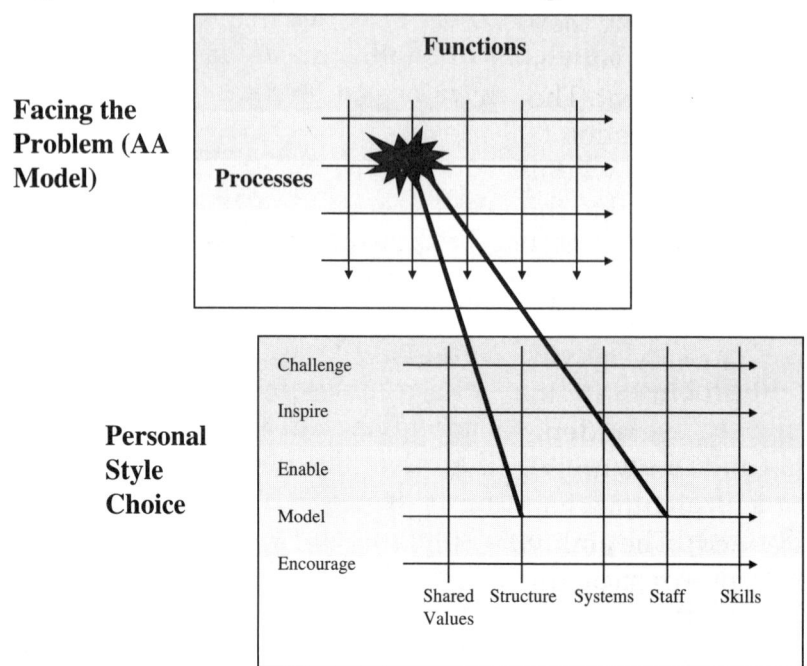

Figure 9-1. A basis for deliberate management action.

Facing the Problem (AA Model)

Functions / Processes

Personal Style Choice

Challenge
Inspire
Enable
Model
Encourage

Shared Values | Structure | Systems | Staff | Skills

Possible Administrative Interventions

have placed style on the vertical axis of the lower chart in Figure 9-1, and integrated the leadership model presented by James Kouzes and Barry Posner in their book *The Leadership Challenge*[3] into this new model of ours. The point is not to be exhaustive, but to remind you of the wide degree of flexibility that you and every leader actually enjoy.

According to Kouzes and Posner, the term *challenge* means to challenge the existing decision-making process. *Inspire* means to share a motivating vision of what can be. *Enabling* means promoting ownership and ensuring that those responsible for making things right have a personal stake in their success. *Modeling* means walking the talk—for example, building large successes on platforms of small positive steps—and then holding yourself as accountable for results as you hold others. *Encouraging* is showing people that they can and will win if they persist, and supporting them while they do so.

Clearly, your style choice and your intervention are interdependent. They depend on the nature of the problem your organization faces, and on the caliber and experience of the people who must resolve the matter. The point is to be flexible and to think about which style to use before you act.

You will notice that as you move from right to left across the chart and all its potential interventions, you are concurrently moving up the executive hierarchy with increased authority to change things. Typically, junior management can redeploy skills within their area of authority, but they have no license to alter their organization's structure. Structural changes are reserved for more senior management. The ability to make changes to corporate culture, strategy, or structure on a grand scale is an exclusive senior management responsibility because it demands commensurate authority to commit the organization to changes of that scope. But you can influence these organizational elements within your own unit.

Many promising executives fail to live up to their potential because they employ a narrow range of styles. They use one style of intervention for every problem they face, and deliver their messages to their organizations through one channel and in one way. Unfortunately, this behavior suggests limitations of intent, strategy, effort, or ability, while the real problem may simply be a personally narrow style range. The transition from arrogant young manager to contentious but constructive executive colleague to decisive leader is a tough road, but it is a transition that only comes to those who widen the array of styles they use to deal with people above, below, and alongside them during their careers.

In contrast, executives described as singularly gifted are those who flexibly choose their administrative and leadership styles carefully from the full array of possibilities. The higher you sit, the wider the choice should be. Hence, we suggest that you consider not just what you will say—the knowledge-based agenda described in this book—but also plan what others will hear and see you doing.

Understanding that Structures Are Expendable but Reorganizations Are Costly

The term *organization* has been the butt of many jokes over the years, suggesting that most of us know that corporations, somehow, get things mixed up and blunder from one form of *mis*-organization to another. One apocryphal tale of this genre concerns a new manager who finds a legacy from his predecessor on his desk on his first day in office—three envelopes numbered one, two and three, with instructions to "Open these in this order when you have real problems."

In due course, things turned awful, so the manager, short of a solution, opened the first envelope and found a piece of paper with the advice, "Blame your predecessor!" Since this advice seemed to work, the manager reached for the second envelope some time later when a new problem appeared to be insurmountable. Again, he found a piece of paper. This one read, "Reorganize!" It too seemed to work. When his third test finally arrived, the manager went again to his desk drawer for the final envelope. This time he read, "Prepare three envelopes!"

This short tale reflects the skepticism that afflicts so many corporations when organization and reorganization are discussed. Nevertheless, organizational structures are expendable. We organize and reorganize to help ourselves achieve our objectives. We have already argued that unless we change our measurement system, our strategy changes will be stillborn. Similarly, unless you change your organization's structure, the likelihood of successfully executing a substantial strategy change is quite low. Because every reorganization is a threat to the power of some individuals and a demand that they change what they do and begin to learn a new job, it is best undertaken voluntarily. It is best pursued when those who will be affected understand its purpose

Several years ago at a large Midwestern company, a senior executive reflected on the realities of many of the reorganizations he had seen. He called them shake-ups. "Every few years we shake the tree here, and all that seems to happen is that the same gulls squawk loudly as they fly off, dump on someone, and land on a higher perch." Take the attention and energy that your management team wastes in an environment of constant organizational shake-ups and apply them to the more fruitful pursuit of your strategy for the future. To do this will take discipline on your part, but the benefits will be well worth the price paid.

Do not shake up your own unit casually, because in doing so, you will be tampering with the informal organization in unknown ways. Yet do not hesitate to reorganize whenever you have determined—following the kinds of approaches described in this book—that such change will help you to address your customers more effectively and efficiently.

Conclusion

Many corporate projects and change initiatives begin with unfounded enthusiasm, but then degenerate into confusion and disappointment as hopes are dashed by events beyond management's apparent control. Cynics have said that such enthusiasm is inevitably followed by confusion, confusion by disappointment, and disappointment by a search for the guilty, coupled with a round of high honors for the uninvolved. Every aspect of such a management system is wrong, the very antithesis of what we have observed as the distinguishing characteristics of the knowing corporation. Throughout this book, we have offered antidotes to this deadly pattern by advocating learning in action to build competencies, expand capabilities, and test your strategies and markets. This type of learning is accelerated by prepared minds and stimulated by new, shared visions of the organization and its environment.

At the business unit level, paradoxically, patience is essential for good timing with markets, executives, and, sometimes, competitors. Confidence founded in knowledge—the only sound basis for commitment—can be your organization's critical foundation for patience. True excellence stems from listening in the broadest sense to the people who manage the company's resources, no matter what their level is. Those at middle and lower levels of the corporate ladder often know what needs to be done.

Finally, at the corporate level, there are a variety of different businesses and enterprises that management leads and joins. Treasure the flexibility these choices give your company. Recognize that, ultimately, advantage is earned by incisively deploying resources, carefully selecting which business processes to own, and when to work in concert with others to satisfy your enterprise's customers, one business at a time.

Knowledge-based consensus, and the plans that it engenders, can replace confusion, disappointment, and cynicism. You are a knowing corporation if your organization turns on cue, as one entity, and achieves its full competitive impact because it is knowledgeable enough to confidently move with dispatch. And you are a knowing leader when you can cause this to happen.

Notes

1. Andrew Grove and Robert Burgleman, "Strategic Dissonance," *California Management Review*, 38:2, 1996, p. 11.
2. Richard T. Pascale and Anthony G. Athos, *The Art of Japanese Management* (New York: Warner Books, 1982).
3. James Kouzes and Barry Posner, *The Leadership Challenge* (San Francisco: Jossey-Bass, 1995), p. 18.

Selected References

This book, although centered on the topic of knowledge management, also includes ideas from other more traditional fields of management. For those who wish to either dig deeper into some of the particular topics dealt with here or gain more understanding of the foundation of some of the ideas in this book, we recommend this list of readings.

Knowledge Management

Thomas Davenport and Laurence Prusak's book, *Working Knowledge: How Organizations Manage What they Know*, HBS Press, 1997, presents a useful introduction to the elements of knowledge generation, codification, and transfer with descriptions of a series of early knowledge management projects. George Von Krogh, Kazuo Ichiro, and Ikujiro Nonaka's book, *Enabling Knowledge Creation*, Oxford University Press, 2000, introduces five generic "enablers" of knowledge creation, aimed at building a cultural foundation to nurture tacit dimensions of knowledge in all places at all times. One of the earliest books about the benefits of learning from action is by Taiichi Ohno, *Toyota Production System: Beyond Large-Scale Production*, Productivity Press, 1988. David Garvin's *Learning in Action: A Guide to Putting the Learning Organization to Work*, Harvard Business School Press, 2000, describes the basic elements of learning organizations, systematically discusses the different modes or processes of learning, and concludes with an exploration of the leadership challenges in building a learning organization.

Process-Engineered Organizations

We present a view of knowledge management that is aimed at operating managers and builds on the strengths that many companies have built through cross-functional business processes. For an early view of how this perspective relates to the new product development process, see Stephen R. Rosenthal, *Effective Product Design and Development*, BusinessOne Irwin (now McGraw-Hill), 1992. For authoritative coverage of the order fulfillment process across organizations in a supply chain, see James P. Womack and Daniel T. Jones, *Lean Thinking*, Simon & Schuster, 1996. For observations about the implementation challenges—emphasizing changes in the nature of work and management—facing companies that wish to move strongly toward the process-centered approach by the pioneer of business process reengineering, see Michael Hammer, *Beyond Reengineering*, Harper Business, 1996. Thomas Davenport's book *Mission Critical: Realizing the Promise of Enterprise Systems,* Harvard Business School Press, 2000, deals with the IT dimension of process-centering and argues that the introduction of enterprise systems will only be successful if the organization simultaneously changes its business processes and strategy.

Customer-Centering

Our view of knowledge management is that it becomes especially powerful in an organization that is focused on understanding its customers and how to serve them at a profit. A classic perspective on customer-centering is the book written by Jan Carlzon when he was president of Scandinavian Airlines, *Moments of Truth*, Harper & Row, 1987. For a more recent statement of this ideal and its best practices, see George S. Day, *The Market Driven Organization: Understanding, Attracting, and Keeping Valuable Customers*, The Free Press, 1997. A process view of how to transform product delivery organizations to deliver higher quality in the eyes of the customer is provided by Fred A. Kuglin in *Customer-Centered Supply Chain Management: A Link-by-Link Guide*, AMACOM, 1998.

Innovation

Knowledge management, as we have dealt with it, is tightly linked with innovation. One of the first systematic treatments of this notion, with an emphasis on the sources of knowledge, was Dorothy Leonard-Barton's *Wellsprings of Knowledge*, Harvard Business School Press, 1995. Andrew Grove's book *Only the Paranoid Survive*, Currency Doubleday, 1996, presents an enlightened CEO's story of how to promote an innovative culture in a company with a great record of past success. In *How the Web Was Won*, Broadway Books, 1999, Paul Andrews presents a detailed look at the process through which Microsoft belatedly became committed to innovation by embracing the Internet.

Business Strategy and Performance Measurement

The two themes in this category that we have emphasized are that strategy needs to be dynamic and that progress toward achieving it needs to be measured. The first of these two themes is covered by Shona Brown and Kathleen Eisenhardt in *Competing on the Edge: Strategy as Structured Chaos*, Harvard Business School Press, 1998, by redefining strategy as charting a course in the awkward zone between anarchy and order. The second, dealing with measures, is covered in depth by Robert S. Kaplan and David P. Norton in *The Balanced Scorecard: Translating Strategy into Action*, Harvard Business School Press, 1996. While concentrating on strategy evaluation, we also touched on issues about the formation of breakthrough business strategies, a subject that is treated with a refreshingly novel framework by Evan M. Dudik in *Strategic Renaissance*, AMACOM, 2000.

Index

AA model, *see* Action Alignment model
AARs (after-action reviews), 9
action, emergence of knowledge from, 10–11
action alignment, 12–13, 19–46
   and achievement of dynamic alignment, 43–45
   advantages of, 26–28
   and assessment of alignments and misalignments, 35–40
   and capabilities, 28–29, 42
   and capability gaps, 29, 42–43
   checking short-term results of, 40–42
   dynamic, 43–45
   as framework for customer-centering, 21–26
   and identification of core processes/functions, 32–35
   and shared knowledge, 30–45
Action Alignment (AA) model, 12–13
   benefits of using, 25–26
   business processes in, 23, 25
   and customers, 27–28
   goal of, 23
   schematic of, 24
   shared knowledge using, 30–45
action-learning process, 207–213
   elements of, 208
   and management, 207–211
   sense of urgency in, 211–212

active listening, 220
after-action reviews (AARs), 9
alignment, 20, 35–37, *see also* action alignment
alliances, business, 150
Amana, 87
Amazon.com, 5–6, 29, 62, 135
Analog Devices Corporation, 181–182
Andersen Corporation, 150–151
Anheuser-Busch, 143–146
APM, *see* Australian Paper Manufacturers
Arthur Andersen, 52
audit team, 31, 38
Australian Paper Manufacturers (APM), 146–148

Balanced Scorecard, 161–162
Bank One Corporation, 148–150
Barnes & Noble, 135
Boeing, 75
Bose, 52
BP (British Petroleum), 8
BPR (business process reengineering), 23
brewing industry, 41–42
British Petroleum (BP), 8
Brown, John, on generating value, 2
B2B, *see* business-to-business
B2C, *see* business-to-consumer

business alliances, 150
business process reengineering (BPR), 23
business-to-business (B2B), 101–102
business-to-consumer (B2C), 101–102

CALL (Center for Army Lessons Learned), 9
Calyx & Corolla, 62–70, 74, 75, 83
capabilities, 28–29, 99–101
 core, 32–33
 improving, 175–177
 process, 42
capability/competency staircase, 99–101
capability gaps, 29, 42–43
capacity, cost of, 72
Caterpillar Inc. (CAT), 79–80
Celestica, 60
Center for Army Lessons Learned (CALL), 9
CEOs, *see* chief executive officers
challenges, 224
chief executive officers (CEOs), 2, 129, 159, 204, 206, 212
Cisco, 52
Colgate-Palmolive, 29
competencies, *see* core competencies; organizational competency(ies)
competency gaps, 50–51, 93–94, 120
competitive advantage, 126–127
consumer-to-consumer (C2C), 101, 102
contract/do decisions, 61, 63, 70–77
contracting out, 61–62, 70–71
convergence, 188
core competencies, 51, 99–101

core processes and functions, identification of, 32–35, 66–68
core rigidities, 203
cost(s)
 of capacity, 72
 of competency gaps, 120
 of customer-centering, 47
 hard vs. soft, 73
credit and collections, 29
cross-functional business processes, 21–22
C2C, *see* consumer-to-consumer
culture, 193–214
 and achievement of transformational change, 195–198
 creating see-screen-search-sign-sell chains in, 198–207
 institutionalizing action-learning process within, 207–213
 making shared knowledge part of, 193–194
 and source of ideas/initiatives, 194–195
customer-centering, 11
 and aligned operations, 26–28
 costs of, 47
 framework for, 21–26
customer pull, 63–64
customer traps, avoiding, 96–98

d'Arbeloff, Alex, 198, 200, 202, 203
deliberate speed, 16–17
Dell, 33–35, 52, 60
Demings, W. Edwards, 27
Disney, 52, 109
do/contract decision, 13
Drucker, Peter, 2, 203
dynamic alignment, achieving, 43–45

Index

earnings per share (eps), 166
ebay, 101–104
e-business ventures, as experiments, 148–150
Edison, Thomas, on experiments, 197
EEC, *see* European Economic Community
EKG reviews, 14–15, 153–157, 202, 218
electronic commerce, 12
electronics industry, 60
emerging technologies, 6
employees, as sources of knowledge, 4
encouraging, 224–225
enterprise leadership, 48–50
enterprises, 47–48
eps (earnings per share), 166
ERP, 60
European Economic Community (EEC), 114, 116
experiments, 4, 137–159
  at Andersen Windows, 150–151
  at Anheuser-Busch, 143–146
  by Australian Paper Manufacturers, 146–148
  at Bank One Corporation, 148–150
  and business alliances, 150
  e-business ventures as, 148–150
  and management, 138–139
  measuring strategic EKG with, 153–157
  operational, 150–151
  and organizational learning, 151–157
  potential benefits of, 139
  questions for driving strategic, 137
  rationale for, 137
  at Steuben Glass, 139–142

successful vs. failed, 138
underutilization of, as strategy, 138
external stockholder constraints, 127–128

Falstaff, 143
Federal Express, 52, 62, 68, 75, 83
finance function, 23, 52
Fuji Xerox, 97

General Electric (GE), 39, 55, 87, 164, 179–180, 182, 193
Georgia Gulf, 108–109
Georgia Pacific, 108
Gerstner, Louis, 195
Gillette, 52
globalization, 7
Grossman, David, 194–195
Grove, Andy
  on listening, 221–222
  on strategic dissonance, 203–204, 206

Hamel, Gary, 194
hard costs, 73
Hastings, Donald, 92, 93
Hewlett-Packard (HP), 29, 131–134
Hewlett-Packard Singapore, 131–134
hollowing out, 72
horizontal thinking, 25
Houghton, Arthur A., Jr., 140–142
HP, *see* Hewlett-Packard
human resources (HR), 52
human resources management (HRM), 23, 38

IBM, 75, 194–195, 221
information technology (IT), 7, 23, 33, 52, 102, 148

Intel, 52, 206–207
internal stockholder constraints,
    128–129
Internet, 12, 48, 66
IT, *see* information technology

Jaybil, 60
JP Morgan, 52

knowing corporations, 7–10
knowledge
    and competitive advantage, 2
    emergence of, from action,
        10–11
    sharing, 3
    stretching with, 3–4
    types of, 2
Kodak, 5
Kouzes, James, 224

Labatt, 143
Laura Ashley, 109–113
LBOs (leveraged buyouts), 108
leadership, 9
    enterprise, 48–50
    and knowledge edge, 16–18
    shift in nature of, 1–2
The Leadership Challenge (James
    Kouzes and Barry Posner),
    224–225
Leonard-Barton, Dorothy, 203
leveraged buyouts (LBOs), 108
Lexus, 29
Lincoln Electric
    knowledge stretches at, 90–95
    organizational competencies of,
        54–56
listening, 220–223

Mackenback, Fred, 92
management information system
    (MIS), 185

marketing, 52
Marks & Spencer, 163–164
McCoy, John B., 148–150
McDonalds, 52
MCI Worldcom, 29
McKinsey & Company, 52, 223
Merck, Robert, 197
metrics, performance, 15, *see also*
    performance measurement
    system
Micron, 52
Microsoft, 5, 155–157
Miller Brewing, 145, 146
misalignments, assessment of,
    36–40
misinformation, 185–187
MIS (management information
    system), 185
modeling, 224
Motorola, 52, 182, 193

networked enterprises, 47–48
new economy, 6–7
new product development, 21, 29,
    64
Nike, 52
Nortel Networks, 150

operations, as functional compe-
    tency, 52
order acquisition, 29, 64
order fulfillment, 29, 64
organizational competency(ies),
    50–59, 135–136
    core competencies vs., 51
    definition of, 50–51
    at Lincoln Electric, 54–56
    and performance measure-
        ment, 177–180
    and 3C balance, 51, 53–59
organizational experiments, *see*
    experiments

Index

organizational learning, 151–157
Otis Elevator, 113–118
Owades, Ruth, 63–66, 68, 69

Patrick, John, 194–195
performance measurement (PM)
  system, 121, 161–191
  assessing current, 163–166
  Balanced Scorecard as, 161–162
  and capability improvements, 175–177
  increasing focus in, 166–173
  and organizational competency, 177–180
  and profitability, 173–174
  and stakeholders, 174–175
  structure of, 165–166
  targeting in, 180–184
  uncovering problems in, 184–189
  usefulness of, 164–165
performance metrics, 15
personal involvement, 215–228
P & G, 52
Pitney Bowes, 98
PM system, *see* performance measurement system
Porter, Michael, 188
Posner, Barry, 224
post-sales service, 29, 64
PP&E (property, plant, and equipment), 71
product development, *see* new product development
profitability, 173–174
property, plant, and equipment (PP&E), 71
"push/pull" exercise, 20

RadioShack, 155
risk, 107–134
  evaluation of, 107–109

inevitability of, 118–123
of not preparing for new stretch strategy, 109–113
successful management of, 114–117

Schlitz, 143, 145
seeking new knowledge, 4, 217
see-screen-search-sign-sell chains, 198–207
Seiff, Marcus, 164
senior management, and business experiments, 138–139, *see also* chief executive officers
shared knowledge, 3, 30–45, 216, *see also* action alignment
  alignments/misalignments as, 35–40
  capabilities/capability gaps as, 42–43
  core functions/processes as, 32–35
  dynamic alignment resulting from, 43–45
short-term results, checking, 40–42
Shreve, Crump, and Low, 140–141
6-sigma quality programs, 193–194
soft costs, 73
Solectron, 52, 60
Sony, 52
staircase (for stretching), 99–101
Stata, Ray, on knowledge, 2
Steuben Glass, 139–142
stockholder constraints
  external, 127–128
  internal, 128–129
strategic dissonance, 203–204
strategic stretch test, 14

stretches, knowledge, 3–4, 79–106, 217, *see also* risk
  asking questions during, 117–118
  and avoidance of customer traps, 96–98
  at Caterpillar, 79–80
  and competency gaps, 93–94
  and competitive advantage/surprise, 126–127
  at deliberate speed, 94–95
  at eBay, 101–104
  evaluation of, 95–96, 104–106
  external stakeholder constraints on, 127–128
  feasibility of, 81–82, 123–130
  go vs. no-go decision regarding, 129–130
  at Hewlett-Packard Singapore, 131–134
  internal stakeholder constraints on, 128–129
  at Lincoln Electric, 90–95
  at Otis Elevator, 113–118
  preparation for, 98–99
  prerequisites for, 80–81
  risk of not preparing for, 109–113
  staircase metaphor for, 99–101
  strategies for, 82–84
  and 3C analysis, 84–90
supply chains, 26

Tandy, 155–157
targeting (in performance management), 180–184

technology(-ies)
  emerging, 6
  as functional competency, 52
Teradyne, 198, 200, 202
3C test for strategic balance, 13–14, 51, 53–59, 68–70
  and knowledge stretches, 84–90
  and resource feasibility, 124, 126
total quality management (TQM), 44
Toyota, 57, 182
TQM (total quality management), 44
transformational change, achievement of, 195–198
Twain, Mark, 120

United States Army, 8–9
UNIX, 198
urgency, sense of, 211–212
USX, 97

The Wall Street Journal, 149
Watson, Thomas, 221
Weatherup, Craig, on creating structured, repeatable processes, 22
Welch, Jack, 39, 164
white spaces, 61–62
Whitman, Meg, 103
Wingspan, 148–150

Xerox, 52, 97